XForms Essentials

Other XML resources from O'Reilly

Related titles

XML in a Nutshell	Practical RDF
Learning XML	XPath and XPointer
XML Pocket Reference	XSL-FO
XSLT	Perl & XML
XSLT Cookbook	Java & XML
XML Schema	Java & XML Data Binding
Web Services Essentials	Java & XSLT
SVG Essentials	Content Syndication with
Programming Web	RSS
Services with SOAP	

XML Books Resource Center

xml.oreilly.com is a complete catalog of O'Reilly's books on XML and related technologies, including sample chapters and code examples.

XML.com helps you discover XML and learn how this Internet technology can solve real-world problems in information management and electronic commerce.

Conferences

O'Reilly & Associates brings diverse innovators together to nurture the ideas that spark revolutionary industries. We specialize in documenting the latest tools and systems, translating the innovator's knowledge into useful skills for those in the trenches. Visit *conferences.oreilly.com* for our upcoming events.

Safari Bookshelf (*safari.oreilly.com*) is the premier online reference library for programmers and IT professionals. Conduct searches across more than 1,000 books. Subscribers can zero in on answers to time-critical questions in a matter of seconds. Read the books on your Bookshelf from cover to cover or simply flip to the page you need. Try it today with a free trial.

XForms Essentials

Micah Dubinko

O'REILLY®

Beijing · Cambridge · Farnham · Köln · Paris · Sebastopol · Taipei · Tokyo

XForms Essentials
by Micah Dubinko

Copyright © 2003 Micah Dubinko. All rights reserved.
Printed in the United States of America.

Published by O'Reilly & Associates, Inc., 1005 Gravenstein Highway North, Sebastopol, CA 95472.

O'Reilly & Associates books may be purchased for educational, business, or sales promotional use. Online editions are also available for most titles (*safari.oreilly.com*). For more information, contact our corporate/institutional sales department: (800) 998-9938 or *corporate@oreilly.com*.

Editor:	Simon St.Laurent
Production Editor:	Reg Aubry
Cover Designer:	Ellie Volckhausen
Interior Designer:	David Futato

Printing History:

August 2003:	First Edition.

ISBN: 0-596-00369-2
[C]

Table of Contents

Preface

The book in your hands introduces you to XForms, a combination of two of the most successful experiments ever performed with the Web: XML and forms.

2003 marks the 10-year anniversary of forms on the Web. During that time, the Web grew from a loose collection of technical research sites to the livelihood of millions, browser empires have risen and fallen, and the tech economy went through an inflationary period of cosmic proportions only to collapse back in upon itself. The addition of forms to the otherwise static HTML language in 1993 was a revolutionary step forward, making possible Yahoo!, Google, Amazon, Hotmail, and countless other interactive sites.

During the mid-nineties, the World Wide Web Consortium (W3C) began work on XML, a uniform way to represent structured text and data, in an attempt to simplify an earlier language called SGML. XML became a W3C Recommendation in 1998, and has since gained momentum, becoming the foundation for XHTML, SVG, the Universal Business Language (UBL), syndication formats such as RSS, and DocBook (which was used to write this book). Nearly every data format that consists primarily of human-readable data has been influenced by XML.

At last, XForms—officially described at *http://www.w3.org/TR/xforms*—provides a way for web forms to serve as XML data collection tools. Increasingly, IT departments are using XML and native XML databases to store mission-critical data. Workflow and routing systems rely on XML for data representation. Web services, which are growing immensely in popularity, are the final piece of the puzzle—making it easy (and providing needed tool support) to send and receive XML data and documents.

Who Should Read This Book?

You should read this book if you want to:

- Create XForms files in a text or XML editor
- Convert existing forms (electronic or paper) to XForms
- Collect XML data from users in a user-friendly way
- Reduce the amount of JavaScript needed within browser interfaces
- Increase the security and reliability of your current information system by combining client-side and server-side checks into a common code base
- Understand how to create interactive web sites using the latest standard technology

Who Should Not Read This Book?

If you simply want to fill out a form, you need only acquire the appropriate software or browser plug-in. There's no need for you to know what's going on behind the scenes unless you wish to satisfy your commendable intellectual curiosity.

If you wish to create forms with a designer program that has XForms export capability, just read that program's documentation to learn how to use that program feature. XForms goes to great lengths to make the fill-out experience intuitive; reading instructions is not required.

If You're Still Reading This...

Form designers tend to come from one of two camps: either graphical design people who find themselves thrust into a world of databases, or technical folks who face the challenge of creating a suitable (and aesthetically pleasing) frontend for their data. This book tends to lean mainly toward the technical side and, in fact, offers very little advice on purely aesthetic issues involved in laying out forms. Some basic knowledge of XML will come in handy, though other W3C technologies used by XForms will be introduced and covered in separate chapters. If you are completely unfamiliar with XML, you will likely benefit by first reading through some of the introductory XML material on the Web, such as at *http://www.xml.com*.

About the Examples

All the examples in this book have been tested with both a commercial and an open source XForms browser, typically Novell XForms Explorer (*http://www.novell.com/xforms*), X-Smiles (*http://www.x-smiles.org*)(from the Helsinki University of Technology), and the FormsPlayer plug-in from X-Port (*http://www.formsplayer.com*).

Organization of This Book

This book is organized into three divisions. The first gives a general introduction to web forms, including information on the history and basic construction of forms. The second section serves as a kind of reference manual to the XForms specification. The third section offers additional hints, guidelines, and techniques for working with XForms.

Chapter 1, *Introduction to Web Forms*
> This chapter gives a brief history of HTML forms and XForms, the design philosophy behind XForms, and some necessary terminology and concepts.

Chapter 2, *XForms Building Blocks*
> Unlike some XML-based languages, XForms is not defined as a standalone document type. This design decision has ramifications that are necessary to understand in order to make effective use of XForms. This chapter discusses issues that come up in the process of defining a markup language (such as XHTML or SVG) that includes XForms.

Chapter 3, *XPath in XForms*
> XPath is another W3C standard that isn't used by itself but in concert with other specifications. XForms is a first-class application of XPath, joining the ranks of XSLT and XPointer. This chapter serves as a complete reference to all of XPath, with particular attention to the parts that are most useful in forms or defined within the XForms specification itself.

Chapter 4, *XML Schema in XForms*
> XML Schema is another W3C technology leveraged by XForms. This chapter gives an overview of the parts of XML Schema that are important for forms and describes the new datatypes introduced by XForms.

Chapter 5, *The XForms Model*

A powerful feature in XForms is the ability to declaratively specify that a form control is required, read-only, calculated, or relevant to the form. The combined definitions of these properties are called the XForms Model, which is the subject of this chapter.

Chapter 6, *The XForms User Interface*

The user interface is the most immediately recognizable part of a form. This chapter discusses the user interface, including details on how the conceptual level of XForms form controls differs from that of HTML form controls.

Chapter 7, *Actions and Events*

This chapter discusses a topic of critical importance to XForms: XML Events. Observing, catching, dispatching, and responding to events remains among the chief reasons for using script with HTML forms. With the advent of XML Events (a separate W3C specification that is finding use in XForms, XHTML, and other places), many functions that used to require script can be written declaratively in XML.

Chapter 8, *Submit*

Nearly every form is intended to submit data at some point. In addition to introducing XML data into forms, XForms defines backward-compatible data submission, as well as a few new tricks. This chapter guides you through all the options, including hints on how to select the appropriate options to match your specific needs.

Chapter 9, *Styling XForms*

XForms forces authors to think about the separation between content and presentation. As a result, specifying style information becomes more important with XForms. This chapter discusses new and existing stylesheet syntax that applies to forms.

Chapter 10, *Form Accessibility, Design, and Troubleshooting*

This chapter includes lots of tips for designing forms for accessibility, so that different users can make full use of the form. Additionally, this chapter includes different techniques and useful design patterns for forms.

Chapter 11, *Extending XForms*

This chapter covers the many ways in which XForms can be extended, including in a future version of XForms that is now underway.

Appendix A, *Examining Microsoft InfoPath*

Microsoft has developed an application called InfoPath that is frequently compared to XForms. This appendix compares some technical aspects of XForms implementations with InfoPath.

Appendix B, *The GNU Free Documentation License*
> This book is being made available under the GNU Free Documentation License, which provides certain freedoms related to copying, modifying, and distributing this book. This appendix contains pointers to the online version of the book (which includes additional examples and errata), as well as the text of the license.

Conventions Used in This Book

`Constant width` is used for code examples, code fragments, XML elements, and attributes.

`Constant width bold` is used to highlight a section of code being discussed in the text.

`Constant width italic` is used for replaceable elements in code examples.

In examples that involve XML Namespaces, the following conventions are used for namespace prefixes:

`html`
> The namespace of XHTML, *http://www.w3.org/1999/xhtml*

`my`
> A prefix that represents an arbitrary user-defined namespace

`xforms`
> The namespace of XForms, *http://www.w3.org/2002/xforms*

`xs`
> The namespace of XML Schema, *http://www.w3.org/2001/XMLSchema*

`xsi`
> The namespace of XML Schema for Instances, *http://www.w3.org/2001/XMLSchema-instance*

How to Contact Us

Please address comments and questions concerning this book to the publisher:

O'Reilly & Associates, Inc.
101 Morris Street Sebastopol, CA 95472
1-800-998-9938 (in the United States or Canada)
1-707-829-0515 (international/local)
1-707-829-0104 (fax)

To comment or ask technical questions about this book, send email to:

bookquestions@oreilly.com

For more information about our books, conferences, software, Resource Centers, and the O'Reilly Network, see our web site at:

http://www.oreilly.com

Acknowledgments

Foremost, thanks to my wife, Ann, and my daughter, Anita, both of whom put up with great stretches of my writing time away from them. Without their support, I never could have made it through the tough times.

I'd also like to thank Simon St.Laurent, the editor of this book, and Edd Dumbill, the editor of xml.com—two of the sharpest XML geeks I've had the pleasure of knowing. Support and encouragement from both of them have helped me improve as a writer and gain the confidence to take on this challenging and rewarding project.

The members of the XForms Working Group have been a tremendous resource, especially the chair, Steven Pemberton, and one of the founders and former chair, Sebastian Schnitzenbaumer. Also, Mikko Honkala from the Helsinki University of Technology and Kenneth Sklander and David Landwehr from Novell have been noteworthy in their sharing of implementation experience on the public mailing list at www-forms@w3.org. Countless other implementers, too many to name, have likewise made valuable contributions.

I also need to thank Richard Stallman: even though I don't agree with him on many things, I do agree that the GNU Free Documentation License that he helped create is a great way to release a technical book such as this one.

One advantage of putting early versions of a book on the Web is the huge amount of feedback you get, even from the earliest stages. Even before formal review, I had the following notice, absolutely true even then, in the preface: "The technical reviewers for this book were amazingly helpful. It was a humbling experience to see just how many mistakes I had inserted into the earlier drafts." Once the formal technical review started, the volume of *quality* comments I received blew away my high expectations. I owe a debt of gratitude to my team of expert reviewers, including Jelks Cabaniss, Stéphane Chauvin, David Ezell, Leigh Klotz, Shane McCarron, Roland Merrick, Mark Seaborne, Jeni Tennison, Eric van der Vlist, and everyone who participated in the xforms-essentials mailing list.

CHAPTER 1

Introduction to Web Forms

*"In the beginning...the earth was without form,
and void."*
—*Genesis 1:1, 2*

How common are forms on the Web? Well, on a recent visit to the news site *http://www.cnn.com*, I counted six separate forms:

1. A navigation list
2. A search tool
3. A stock quote tool
4. A language picker
5. A community poll
6. A weather forecast tool

As a general rule, the more interactive a web site is, the more heavily the site's designers rely on web forms, a general term for all different kinds of technologies used to gather information from users. It is easy to see why this is the case—without forms, web sites are far less interesting. Form-less web sites were the norm in the early days of the Web and provided a one-way deluge of static information, similar to the Sunday newspaper, which requires lots of navigation to get to any specific part and contains countless pages that get printed but never read.

The addition of forms to Hypertext Markup Language (HTML), the primary language used in web pages, launched an entirely new way of surfing the Web. In this book, I use the term *HTML forms* to refer to the form element and related markup from either HTML or XHTML. Using HTML forms, searching for information became possible on a worldwide scale. Sites such as Yahoo! quickly became the most popular "portals" of entry on the Web. Later, as developers pushed the limits of forms technology farther, web sites became even more interactive and customizable. In return for a small piece of information, such as a postal code, the browsing experience could be reshaped to include what specific information visitors were looking for—leaving out the rest. HTML forms have proven so successful in this regard that newer web technologies, such as PDF forms and Flash, have been unable to make a significant dent in their popularity.

The Past, Present, and Future of Web Forms

Scientists and science fiction writers have long predicted many of the things now being made possible by web forms. For example, in a 1945 article in *The Atlantic Monthly*, Vannevar Bush wrote about a hypertext network he dubbed a "Memex." Even at this conceptual stage, the thought of using forms to access data came naturally, particularly in terms of drilling down through vast stores of information: "One might, for example, speak to a microphone, in the manner described in connection with the speech-controlled typewriter, and thus make his selections." How did such a technology come to be in real life?

Shortly after the initial tempering of HTML, various individuals began considering the usefulness of forms alongside hypertext. HTML Version 2.0, as presented in a document called Request for Comments (RFC) 1866, was the first time that web forms were seriously considered for standardization. That RFC captured HTML as found in common use prior to June 1994. At this point, HTML already included forms, thanks to a 1993 proposal called HTML+.

Care and maintenance of the HTML family of specifications have since been handed over to the World Wide Web Consortium, or W3C. The last non-XML-based version of HTML was version 4.01, which didn't change forms processing much. New development of the standard is taking place on a closely related technology called XHTML, where the X indicates an XML foundation. XHTML 1.0 and 1.1 were largely concerned with details of the transition to XML and ways to combine vocabularies, not with major changes to the language.

XHTML 2.0, in contrast, is making some improvements that aren't compatible with earlier flavors of HTML. The largest such change is the adoption of XForms as a replacement for the older HTML forms technology. As of August 2003, XHTML 2.0 is still under development, though it's clear that XForms will play a major role in the future of XHTML. Before we discuss XForms, however, a review of the older HTML forms technology will be helpful.

A Brief Review of HTML Forms

The introduction of the forms chapter in HTML 4.01 reads: "An HTML form is a section of a document containing normal content, markup, special elements called controls (checkboxes, radio buttons, menus, etc.), and labels on those controls. Users generally 'complete' a form by modifying its controls (entering text, selecting menu items, etc.), before submitting the form to an agent for processing (e.g., to a web server, to a mail server, etc.)."

The defining element for HTML forms is named, not too surprisingly, form. This element describes some important aspects of the form, including where and how to submit data. The content of this element consists of regular HTML markup, as well as controls.

Forms represent a structured exchange of data. In HTML forms, the structure of the collected data, called a *form data set*, is a set of name/value pairs. The names and values that are included in this set are solely determined by the controls present within the form, so that adding a new control element, as well as adding to the user interface, also adds a new name/value pair to the data set. Many authors take for granted this basic violation of the separation between the data layer and the user interface layer—a problem that XForms has gone to considerable lengths to alleviate.

Which control types are available in HTML forms? The following sections will answer this question.

Single-Line Text Input

The workhorse of HTML forms, this control permits the entry of any character data. Text input controls accept a string value and contribute it to the form data set. Example 1-1 shows the XHTML code needed to produce a basic single-line text control, and Figure 1-1 shows the result.

Example 1-1. XHTML code for a single-line text control

```
<input type="text" name="name" value="Dubinko, Micah"/>
```

Dubinko, Micah

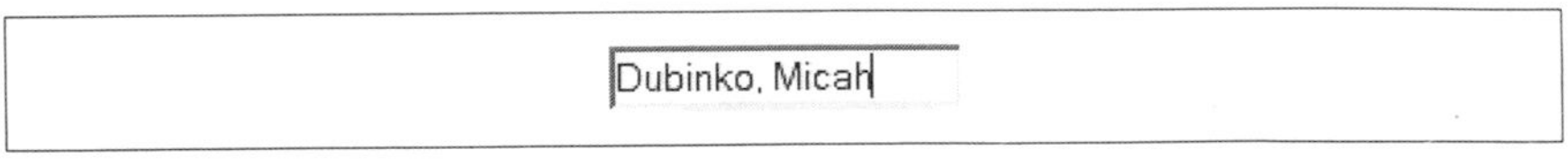

Figure 1-1. Rendering of a single-line text input

Multi-Line Text Input

A more complex variation of text entry is when multiple lines of text need to be entered. For this purpose, HTML forms includes a separate form control that is typically larger than standard text input controls and offers special handling of multiple-line text. Multi-line text input controls contribute to the form data set exactly as do single-line text input controls. Example 1-2 shows the XHTML code for a multi-line text control, and Figure 1-2 shows the result.

Example 1-2. XHTML code for a multi-line text control

```
<textarea name="blogentry">&lt;strong&gt;The Joy of Named ...</textarea>
```

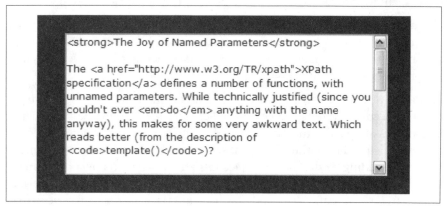

Figure 1-2. Rendering of a multi-line text control

Password Text Input

Another variation of text entry is for sensitive data, such as a password, that could be harmful to display on the screen where someone could "shoulder surf," or covertly observe, and thus compromise security measures. It is important to note that this control provides only a casual level of security in the presentation: it does not, for example, provide any data encryption. Password text input controls contribute to the form data set exactly as do text input controls. Example 1-3 shows the XHTML code needed for a password control, and Figure 1-3 shows the result.

Example 1-3. XHTML code for a password control

```
<input type="password" name="pass"/>
```

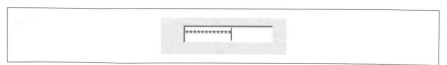

Figure 1-3. Rendering of a password control

Submit and Reset

These controls are similar to buttons, but when activated have the effect of built-in processing (to submit or reset the form, respectively). Reset controls aren't supposed to contribute to the form data set, but up to one submit button can. This can be useful, when there are multiple submit buttons, in determining which one initiated the submission process. Example 1-4 shows the XHTML code needed for submit and reset controls, and Figure 1-4 shows the result.

Example 1-4. XHTML code for submit and reset controls

```
<input type="submit" value="Continue"/>
<!-- also possible <button type="submit"/> or <input type="image"/> -->
<input type="reset" value="Clear Order Form"/>
<!-- also possible <button type="reset"/> -->
```

Figure 1-4. Rendering of submit and reset controls

Buttons

The effect of activating a button is to invoke a call in a scripting language. A button can be specified in two slightly different ways, with the button syntax being slightly more expressive. If a value is assigned to the button, it will be contributed unchanged to the form data set (not the most useful functionality, but there if you need it). Example 1-5 shows the XHTML code for a button control, and Figure 1-5 shows the result.

Example 1-5. XHTML code for a button control

```
<input type="button" value="Calculate"/>
<!-- also possible <button>Calculate</button> -->
```

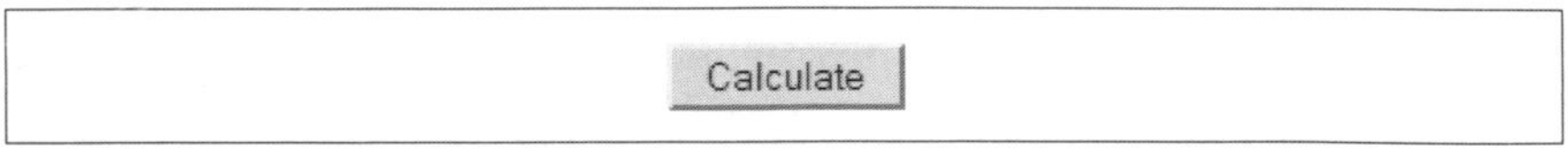

Figure 1-5. Rendering of a button control

Radio Buttons

Named after the mechanical controls on old radios, this common control requires that a single option always be selected, and thus is almost always used as a group of controls with the same name. The HTML specification encourages authors to ensure that a particular choice is initially selected, but in practice authors usually don't select a particular choice, resulting in "undefined" behavior. (One common implementation choice is to provide a temporary exception to the one-thing-must-always-be-selected rule, but it isn't safe to rely on this behavior.) A group of radio buttons provides a single value representing the current selection to the form data set. Example 1-6 shows the XHTML code for a radio button group, and Figure 1-6 shows the result.

Example 1-6. XHTML code for a radio button group

```
<input type="radio" name="car" value="0"/> None<br/>
<input type="radio" name="car" value="1"/> 1 car<br/>
<input type="radio" name="car" value="2"/> 2 cars<br/>
<input type="radio" name="car" value="3"/> 3 cars<br/>
<input type="radio" name="car" value="4"/> 4 cars<br/>
<input type="radio" name="car" value="many"/> 5 or more<br/>
```

```
                          ⊙ None
                          ⊙ 1 car
                          ⊙ 2 cars
                          ⊙ 3 cars
                          ⊙ 4 cars
                          ⊙ 5 or more
```

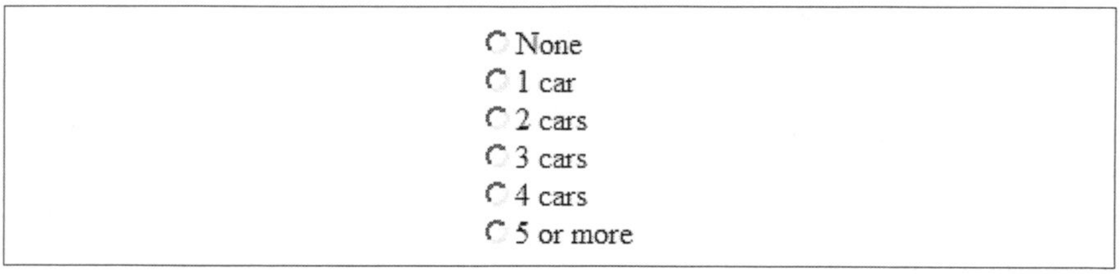

Figure 1-6. Rendering of a radio button group

Checkboxes

This simple on/off control has become familiar to computer users everywhere. Often, this control is used in a group which uses the same name, which allows for a select-zero-or-more behavior, though solo checkboxes are common as well. Only checkboxes that are checked contribute to the form data set. In cases where multiple checkboxes share the same name and are checked, the form data set will contain multiple entries with the same name and each selected value. Example 1-7 shows the XHTML code for a checkbox group, and Figure 1-7 shows the result.

Example 1-7. XHTML code for a checkbox group

```
<input type="checkbox" name="referBy" value="td"/> Test driven a vehicle<br/>
<input type="checkbox" name="referBy" value="dlr"/> Visited an autotmotive
dealer<br/>
<input type="checkbox" name="referBy" value="veh"/> Purchased/Leased a
vehicle<br/>
<input type="checkbox" name="referBy" value="ins"/> Purchased automobile
insurance<br/>
```

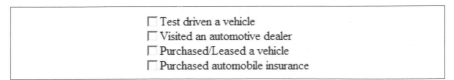

Figure 1-7. Rendering of a checkbox group

Single-Select Menus

Commonly called a *listbox* or *drop-down menu*, this control enforces a single selection out of several options. In effect, this control provides another way to achieve the same function as radio buttons, but with a different visual presentation. As is the case with radio buttons, an initial state that doesn't explicitly select some initial choice is "undefined," though existing implementations usually allow an initial nothing-selected state. Single-select menus use one option child element for each option, which can include both a display value and a storage value. The storage value representing the current selection is provided to the form data set. Example 1-8 shows the XHTML code for a single-select control, and Figure 1-8 shows the result.

Example 1-8. XHTML code for a single-select control

```
<select name="searchtype">
  <option selected="selected" value="all">all words</option>
  <option value="any">any words</option>
</select>
```

all words ▾

Figure 1-8. Rendering of a single-select control

Multiple-Select Menus

Adding an attribute to the select element enables the control to accept multiple selections, or even to select nothing at all. In this configuration, this control can achieve the same function as a group of checkbox controls, but with a different presentation. As with checkboxes, if any options are selected, this control provides the display value of each selection to the form data set. Example 1-9 shows the XHTML code for a multiple-select control, and Figure 1-9 shows the result.

Example 1-9. XHTML code for a multiple-select control

```
<select multiple="multiple">
  <option value="0">UNCONFIRMED</option>
  <option selected="selected" value="1">NEW</option>
  <option selected="selected" value="2">ASSIGNED</option>
```

Example 1-9. XHTML code for a multiple-select control (continued)

```
<option selected="selected" value="3">REOPENED</option>
<option value="4">RESOLVED</option>
<option value="5">VERIFIED</option>
<option value="6">CLOSED</option>
</select>
```

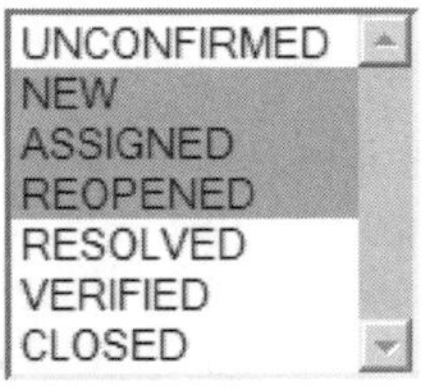

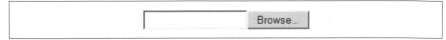

Figure 1-9. Rendering of a multiple-select control

File Select

A more recent addition to HTML was the ability to select a local file to submit along with the rest of the form data. This control contributes binary data into the form data set, which has implications on the wire format used to submit data, as discussed later. The filename selected is also included, in a secondary way, in the submitted data. Example 1-10 shows the XHTML code for a file select control, and Figure 1-10 shows the result.

Example 1-10. XHTML code for a file select control

```
<input type="file" name="attachment"/>
```

Figure 1-10. Rendering of a file select control

Hidden Controls

Often, a form needs to hold more data than what is visible, in order to track state or earlier interactions. This control has no user interface effect, but contributes to the form data set. Example 1-11 shows the XHTML code for a hidden control.

Example 1-11. XHTML code for a hidden control

```
<input type="hidden" name="sessionID"/>
```

Object Controls

Finally, the HTML specification defines a way for additional controls, such as plug-ins or Java applets, to participate in forms. This approach, however, never gained popularity, although clever programmers have used scripting and dynamic HTML to accomplish many of the same goals.

Labels and Legends

Printed forms make extensive use of labels as directions for filling out the document, which is good, since most people don't read the regular instructions, anyway. HTML forms are no different. A label element can be associated with any control, either by wrapping the label around the control, or by referencing an ID unique to the form control. When connected this way, the label becomes an extension of the control, which helps make forms more usable. For example, a radio button label is a much easier target to click on than the tiny circular control itself. When the label is properly connected, clicking it has the same effect as clicking the related control.

Nobody is sure exactly why, but the simple practice of using label elements has failed to catch on with authors. As a result, many HTML forms still use tables and other inaccessible techniques where text associated with a form control might visually appear nearby the control, but is actually defined in some unrelated markup structure, such as a different table cell. That kind of document is a major obstacle for non-visual users to figure out, since the visual proximity of items is the only connection between form controls and labels.

Groups of radio buttons pose another problem for labeling. Each radio button can have an individual label, but what about labeling the overall group? For this purpose, HTML forms include a general-purpose grouping element called fieldset, the first child of which may be legend, which is another kind of label. Example 1-12 shows the XHTML code for a fieldset, and Figure 1-11 shows the result.

Example 1-12. XHTML code for a fieldset

```
<fieldset>
  <legend>Personal Information</legend>
  <input type="radio" name="mstatus" value="M"/> Married<br/>
  <input type="radio" name="mstatus" value="S"/> Single<br/>
  <input type="radio" name="mstatus" value="X"/> Decline to state<br/>
</fieldset>
```

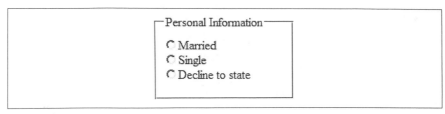

Figure 1-11. Rendering of a fieldset

Access and Navigation

Using a keyboard to get around in a form is not only an accessibility feature, but also a convenience for people who need to fill large numbers of forms or lengthy forms. All controls accept two attributes to help define a keyboard interface:

accesskey
> Defines a character that can be used in conjunction with a system-dependent key (**Alt** on Windows, **Cmd** on Mac, etc.), in order to navigate directly to a particular form control.

tabindex
> Taken as a whole, tabindex attributes form a navigation sequence over the form. Thus, pressing Tab or Shift+Tab brings you to the next or previous control.

Readonly and Disabled

Often it is necessary in an electronic form to have a control that displays, but doesn't allow changes to, a piece of data. This can be accomplished through an attribute called readonly, which unfortunately only applies to text input controls. When a control is read-only, it is still possible to navigate to it, and any data present will still be submitted.

The disabled attribute enforces a stronger prohibition. Any control, even lists, radio buttons, or checkboxes, can be disabled, in which case the browser gives the control a distinctive "grayed out" appearance, indicating its unavailability. It is not possible to navigate to a disabled control, nor will it participate in data submission. Effectively, the control is not part of the form anymore (although it is still available to scripting).

Initialization

Except for the file upload control, it's possible to provide initial data for all form controls, but keeping track of the differing form control types is complicated. Here are some of the different control types and the data they accept:

Textual controls (but not textarea*)*
> Take a value attribute containing a string value

textarea *element*
> Accepts characters as element content

List controls
> Use a selected (or selected="selected" in XHTML) attribute on one or more of the option elements

Radio buttons and checkboxes
> Use a checked (or checked="checked" in XHTML) attribute on one or more of the input elements

Inserting initial data is a major bottleneck in large-scale projects involving forms, both in terms of processing time and in opportunities for bugs to appear. The typical approach is to have a template language that is processed by an application server, effectively doing a large search-and-replace operation before delivering every page containing forms. Workflow and routing scenarios, where submitted data is sent from one user's desktop to another, are similarly burdened with large amounts of templating and tricks to populate forms in advance.

Submit

Usually, the primary purpose of a form is to submit data. The original, and still most popular, encoding for this is called *urlencoded*, and is represented by the Internet media type application/x-www-form-urlencoded. In this encoding, spaces become plus signs, and any other reserved characters become encoded as a percent sign and hexadecimal digits, as defined in RFC 1738. One unfortunate aspect of this definition is that it doesn't describe how to encode anything beyond simple ASCII characters. Some implementations have used the document encoding to control this process, but interoperability has remained elusive.

A second encoding became necessary with the introduction of the file upload control and the binary data this introduced into the form data set. This is called multipart/form-data, and is based on the MIME format defined in RFC 2388. This format allows for much more efficient representation of binary and non-ASCII data.

One final consideration in form submission is *how* the data gets submitted. The HTML specification defines submission through the HTTP methods GET and POST and also includes an example of email, through the mailto:

URI scheme. The HTTP specification gives some specific advice on when to use GET versus POST, which we will consider later.

Example 1-13 shows a simple, but typical, HTML form. Figure 1-12 shows how this form is rendered.

Example 1-13. XHTML code for a typical XHTML form

```
<form action="http://example.com/cgi-bin/submit-here" name="shake-poll">
  <p>Poll: to be or not to be?</p>
  <input type="radio" name="thequestion" id="radio1" value="b"/>
  <label for="radio1">To Be<label><br/>
  <input type="radio" name="thequestion" id="radio2" value="n"/>
  <label for="radio2">Not To Be<label><br/>
  <input type="radio" name="thequestion" id="radio3"/>
  <label for="radio3">Other (please specify)<label><br/>
  <input type="text" name="othersel"/>
</form>
```

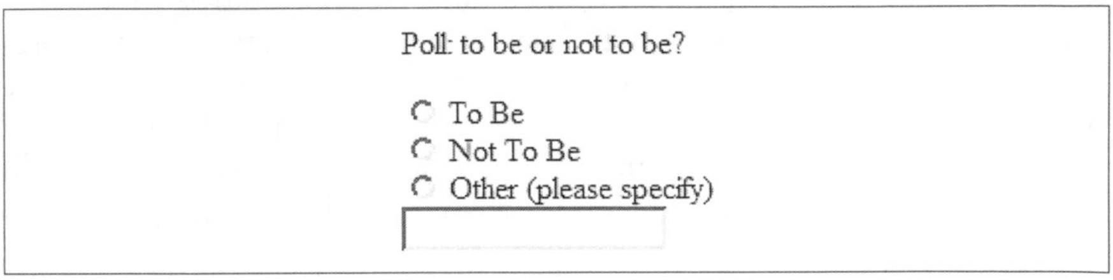

Poll: to be or not to be?

    ○ To Be
    ○ Not To Be
    ○ Other (please specify)

Figure 1-12. Rendering of a typical XHTML form

Limitations of HTML Forms, Advantages of XForms

According to developers, the most commonly cited problem with HTML forms is their dependency on scripting languages. Real-world HTML forms are reliant on script to accomplish many common tasks such as marking controls as required, performing validations and calculations, displaying error messages, and managing dynamic layout. This dependency results in complex documents, which are expensive and time-consuming to maintain, since a full-time programmer is practically necessary when dealing with that much script.

XForms helps reduce the need for script in several ways: by defining a framework for simple, XPath-based calculations and validations, by providing better user feedback on the status of the form, through dynamic features such as repeating tables and optional sections, and through a system of *XForms Actions*—elements that cause commonly needed actions such as setting focus or changing a data value.

A second limitation of HTML forms is the difficulty of initializing form data, as commonly happens when web sites "remember" past users and provide them the courtesy of not having to repeatedly enter information. As shown earlier, each form control has its own unique way of defining initial data, with small bits of initialization data spread all across the document. This means that in order to process a blank form into a filled form, either a new document needs to be constructed piece by piece, or an existing document needs to be patched in numerous places—one of the reasons why template-replacement facilities are commonly found in application servers. Constructing such forms is CPU-intensive and leads to bottlenecks on high-volume servers.

In XForms, form data is provided from an initial XML file, which can be external to the form definition. Since XForms is also flexible enough to deal directly with most XML data formats, piping initial data into a form is typically a simple matter of pointing a src attribute to an existing XML data source.

A third limitation of HTML forms is that the encoding formats, urlencoded or multipart, represent only "flat" data, or name/value pairs. Many types of forms, including purchase orders, would benefit from a richer data representation.

XML is a better foundation for most business documents than a flattened set of names and values. Since it has XML support as a fundamental requirement, XForms excels at helping users create those kinds of documents.

More subtle, but still serious, is a fourth fundamental design flaw in HTML forms: a hidden assumption of a one-step process—from a client to a server—with processing finishing there. In the real world, forms often travel in more complicated paths. For example, a vacation request form might go to a supervisor for approval, then to the human resources department, and finally to accounting for final processing. Managing HTML forms in such a workflow scenario involves reinterpreting the data format at every stage. Perhaps this is one reason why HTML forms aren't commonly seen in use for workflow.

XForms enables a different pattern: it allows form data, as an XML file, to be routed to various workstations, as needed. At each stop, the data is loaded into a form, which provides a viewport into editing all or parts of the document, and submitted again. This process can be repeated as many times as necessary, with any number of participants.

As the HTML Working Group became increasingly aware of the limitations inherent in HTML forms, they decided that they needed to develop a new, non-backward-compatible specification for web forms. To do this, they formed a subgroup (which later became a full Working Group) to define the requirements and begin the initial design work of XForms. They set out to produce a system that would fulfill the following requirements:

- XForms should use XML, both for initial data and submitted data.
- The difference between a blank form and a filled-out form should be minimal and representable as an XML document.
- Forms should be easy to route to multiple users and locations.
- XForms should separate purpose, presentation, and form data. Earlier, each section describing an HTML form control had to define two things: how the control looked, and how it affected the form data set. XForms should cleanly separate these two aspects.
- XForms should provide the 20 percent of functionality needed to avoid 80 percent of all forms scripting.
- Popular features such as calculations and validations should be included in the language.
- XForms should be designed in such a way to encourage those using HTML forms to switch over by making sure that all the commonly used features in HTML forms are still possible in XForms.

The History of XForms

After a number of internal and published requirements documents, the first XForms draft specification was published on April 6, 2000. The title of this document, "Datamodeling Proposal for XForms," gave a strong hint about how undeveloped this initial effort was. In fact, the final versions of the XForms specification bear no resemblance at all to this first attempt.

Why was this? At the time the initial XForms Working Draft was under development, another W3C specification called "XML Schema" was gradually progressing through the W3C channels. In what later proved to be a costly diversion, the XForms Working Group initially decided to make the XForms data types differ from the ones in XML Schema, "due to different usage scenarios and target audiences." As an alternative, the specification spelled out a "simple syntax," which consisted of a number of XML tags such as string, money, and group, where the tags needed to be nested in a structure that mirrored the desired shape of the final XML that would be submitted. For example, to submit XML that looked like:

```
<poll>
  <vote>Vanilla</vote>
</poll>
```

You would have needed an XForms "data model" such as this:

```
<xform>
  <group name="poll">
    <string name="vote">
  </group>
</xform>
```

XForms Terminology

The XForms specification introduces a number of new terms, but a few are especially troublesome from a writer's viewpoint.

form

> As the next two chapters will show, XForms doesn't package everything neatly inside a single element, such as form. Instead, separate pieces can be defined, in different places, and sometimes in different documents. Because of this, it is difficult to use the term "form" in anything other than a broad, generic sense.

field

> The HTML forms specification uses this term casually in a few places, but never formally defines it. In fact, people in the computer and Internet industry have widely diverging opinions on what a field is. Part of a database? Part of a user interface? One could argue for either definition (or both). In the end, the XForms Working Group decided that the term was too overloaded and generally should be avoided when talking about XForms.

XForm (singular)

> For the reasons listed above, the XForms Specification, as well as this book, avoids defining or using the term XForm, as in "To create an XForm, you start by..."

XForms (singular or plural)

> The XForms Working Group public page contains the following note from the editor: "XForms is a word with no singular form. Other such words in the English language are: ALMS, CATTLE, CLOTHES, PLIERS, SCISSORS, and SHORTS." Thus, when referring to the collective noun form, one should say "XForms simplified my web application." When using XForms as shorthand for "the XForms specification," however, it should still be properly treated as a singular noun.

Although avoiding all traces of XML Schema was attractive to some, it proved to be more trouble than it was worth for a W3C specification. Thus, on August 15, 2000, a very brief Working Draft was published, containing not the XForms specification but, rather, the message: "The Working Group is currently studying how to support forms where the data model is defined by an XML Schema plus form specific properties. The previous version of the XForms Data Model is being obsoleted while this work is underway."

The December 2000 and February 2001 Working Drafts expanded on this new direction, and rolled into the document the XForms User Interface and other pieces that were initially conceived as separate specifications. (The final version of the specification defines modules that have much the same effect.) One other notable aspect of these documents is that they contain the first reference to the *XForms Model*, or the core definition of a form independent of any user interface. And, of course, XML Schema datatypes made their appearance, though simple syntax clung on as an extra section.

By the publication of the June 2001 Working Draft, people were starting to gain more experience with XForms authoring. With this experience came the realization that the simple syntax wasn't actually simplifying matters. The core problem was that the simple syntax was required to redundantly mirror the structure of the instance data, or initial XML used as form data, forcing authors in many cases to create the same structure twice in slightly different ways. Even worse, it created interoperability problems between XML-Schema-XForms and simple-syntax-XForms. So out went the simple syntax. XML Schema datatypes turned out to not be that bad after all, and the initial instance data itself held all the structural information needed. Things were starting to look up. In short, this Working Draft was the first to strongly represent the final XForms specification.

A few more publication cycles followed in August and December 2001. These updates consisted mostly of editorial work, though a few notable new features included script interfaces to interact with instance data and a cleaned-up processing model. This led the way for the January 2002 "Last Call" Working Draft, and the associated call for public review of XForms. In five weeks, the public mailing list for comments received around 150 substantive comments—each of which needed to be discussed and given a response. Comments ranged from the aesthetic ("please use only lowercase tag names") to the technical ("don't deprecate the HTTP GET method") to the political ("don't publish again until you have a test suite"). Often different submitters made contradictory requests. All in all, it took several months, and an additional publication in August 2002, for the XForms Working Group to sort through all of the advice, make the necessary changes, and send responses to each comment, as required by the W3C process.

Finally, in November 2002, the XForms Candidate Recommendation was released, along with a call for implementations. Strong support from business and open source implementers, collected at a meeting in February 2003, helped identify pieces of the specification that were hard to implement. As of this writing in August 2003, XForms has reached the Proposed Recommendation stage, and is poised to become a final W3C Recommendation shortly thereafter.

The Revenge of the Simple Syntax

The XForms "simple syntax" mentioned earlier served a worthy purpose: to make authors of existing HTML forms comfortable enough to consider making the jump to XForms. So, when the "simple syntax" went away, what replaced it? Literally nothing. Instead of trying to simplify form authoring by adding an additional layer of markup, the designers made XForms remain useful when *removing* a layer of markup. This extra layer is what needs to be written for the XForms Model, which can be safely omitted in forms of roughly the same complexity as an HTML form with no script. Unofficially, this became known as "lazy author" processing, in deference to the time-honored concept in software engineering of "constructive laziness," or the ability to recognize and actively bypass unnecessary work.

Example 1-14 shows a form that accomplishes the same goals as the earlier HTML form: a poll.

Example 1-14. A poll form implemented in XForms,"lazy author" style

```
<select1 ref="mainsel" appearance="radio" selection="open">
  <label>Poll: to be or not to be?</label>
    <item>
     <label>To Be</label>
     <value>b</value>
    </item>
    <item>
     <label>Not To Be</label>
     <value>n</value>
    </item>
</select1>
```

Note that no specific choice is needed for an "Other, please specify" selection, since XForms supports the concept of "open selection" lists, where the user is allowed to freely enter additional list values.

Additionally, to make the form submittable, a small bit of markup is required in the head section of the document, as seen in the following code.

```
<model>
  <submission action="http://example.info/xml-submit"/>
</model>
```

Unlike the proposed simple syntax, only a minimal amount of keyboard typing is needed for the XForms Model; in fact, little more than a URL to accept submitted data. The main part of the form is specified as user interface form controls: here, select1. Note, too, that the "Other, please specify" choice isn't needed, since XForms supports open selection lists natively. If the user manually entered both as a choice, the resulting XML submitted would look like this:

```
<instanceData>
  <mainsel>both</mainsel>
</instanceData>
```

On the other hand, if the user accepted the initial choice, the shorter storage value given in the value attribute would be used:

```
<instanceData>
  <mainsel>b</mainsel>
</instanceData>
```

While the lazy author syntax saves typing, it also is severely limited in power, lacking any kind of calculation or validation structure. For this reason, the XForms specification encourages form authors to use the full capacity of XForms. The following chapters describe how to do this.

CHAPTER 2

XForms Building Blocks

*"What the world really needs is more love and
less paperwork."*
—-Pearl Bailey

*"XML lets organizations benefit from structured,
predictable documents. Thus, XML breeds forms.
QED."*
—-David Weinberger

The previous chapter ended with a look at the simple syntax of XForms. This chapter goes into greater detail on the concepts underlying the design of XForms, as well as practical issues that come into play, including a complete, annotated real-world example.

A key concept is the relationship between forms and documents, which will be addressed first. After that, this chapter elaborates on the important issue of host languages and how XForms integrates them.

More Than Forms

Despite the name, XForms is being used for many applications beyond simple forms. In particular, creating and editing XML-based documents is a good fit for the technology.

A key advantage of XML-based documents over, say, paper or word processor templates, is that an entirely electronic process eliminates much uncertainty from form processing. Give average "information workers" a paper form, and they'll write illegibly, scribble in the margins, doodle, write in new choices, and just generally do things that aren't expected. All of these behaviors are manually intensive to patch up, in order to clean the data to a point where it can be placed into a database. With XForms, it is possible to restrict the parts of the document that a user is able to modify, which means that submitted data needs only a relatively light double-check before it can be sent to a database. (One pitfall to avoid, however, is a system that is excessively restrictive, so that the person filling the form is unable to accurately provide the needed data. When that happens, users typically give bad information or avoid the electronic system altogether.)

Various efforts are underway to define XML vocabularies for all sorts of documents. Perhaps one of the most ambitious is UBL, the Universal Business Language, currently being standardized through OASIS (the Organization for the Advancement of Structutured Information Standards). The goal of UBL is to represent all different sorts of business documents—purchase orders, invoices, order confirmations, and so on—using a family of XML vocabularies. XForms is a great tool with which to create and edit UBL documents.

A Real-World Example

As an example, this section will develop an XForms solution for creating and editing a UBL purchase order. The first step is to define the initial instance data, which is a skeleton XML document that contains the complete structure of the desired final document, but with only initial data. This document serves as a template for newly-created purchase orders, and provides a framework on which to hang the rest of the form.

 This complete example form is available online at *http://dubinko.info/writing/xforms/ubl/*.

Example 2-1 shows what a UBL purchase order document looks like. Figure 2-1 shows, in the X-Smiles browser, an XForms document capable of creating such a document.

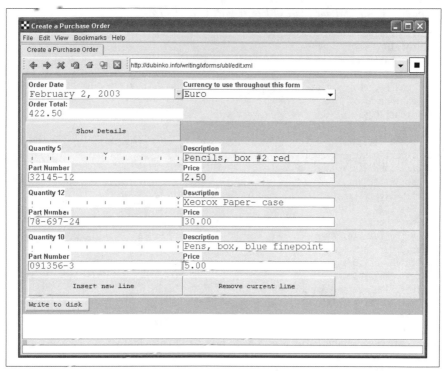

Figure 2-1. An XML purchase order being created with XForms

Example 2-1. An XML purchase order using UBL

```
<Order xmlns="urn:oasis:names:tc:ubl:Order:1.0:0.70"
xmlns:cat="urn:oasis:names:tc:ubl:CommonAggregateTypes:1.0:0.70">
  <cat:ID/>
  <cat:IssueDate/>
  <cat:LineExtensionTotalAmount currencyID="USD"/>
  <cat:BuyerParty>
    <cat:ID/>
    <cat:PartyName>
      <cat:Name/>
    </cat:PartyName>
    <cat:Address>
      <cat:ID/>
      <cat:Street/>
      <cat:CityName/>
      <cat:PostalZone/>
      <cat:CountrySub-Entity/>
    </cat:Address>
    <cat:BuyerContact>
      <cat:ID/>
      <cat:Name/>
    </cat:BuyerContact>
  </cat:BuyerParty>
```

Example 2-1. An XML purchase order using UBL (continued)

```
<cat:SellerParty>
  <cat:ID/>
  <cat:PartyName>
    <cat:Name/>
  </cat:PartyName>
  <cat:Address>
    <cat:ID/>
    <cat:Street/>
    <cat:CityName/>
    <cat:CountrySub-Entity/>
  </cat:Address>
</cat:SellerParty>
<cat:DeliveryTerms>
  <cat:ID/>
  <cat:SpecialTerms/>
</cat:DeliveryTerms>
<cat:OrderLine>
  <cat:BuyersID/>
  <cat:SellersID/>
  <cat:LineExtensionAmount currencyID=""/>
  <cat:Quantity unitCode="">1</cat:Quantity>
  <cat:Item>
    <cat:ID/>
    <cat:Description>Enter description here</cat:Description>
    <cat:SellersItemIdentification>
      <cat:ID>Enter part number here</cat:ID>
    </cat:SellersItemIdentification>
    <cat:BasePrice>
      <cat:PriceAmount currencyID="">0.00</cat:PriceAmount>
    </cat:BasePrice>
  </cat:Item>
</cat:OrderLine>
</Order>
```

The markup used by UBL seems slightly verbose, but this is necessary to capture all the small variations that occur in the purchase orders used by different organizations. Note that the cat:OrderLine element can repeat as many times as necessary, though only a single occurrence is needed for the initial instance data. Also note that the root element uses a different XML namespace than the rest of the document. Thanks to the context node rules in XForms, the root element never needs to be directly referred to, and thus form authors can happily ignore this minor detail.

The next step is to create an XForms document that will serve to edit the initial instance data. XForms itself does not define a document format. Instead, a host language such as XHTML or SVG, combined with XForms, needs to be used. As of this writing, XHTML 2.0, which natively includes XForms, is progressing through the W3C Recommendation track. This example, however, uses the established XHTML 1.1, with XForms elements inserted in the appropriate places. As a result, this example will not validate against any XHTML DTD. Even so, it is still XML well-formed, and browsers that understand XForms presently do a good job rendering this document.

The latter part of this chapter describes complications that occur when combining vocabularies; the opening lines of the XForms document shown in Example 2-2 provide a foregleam, using an arcane XML syntax called an *internal DTD subset* to declare certain attributes as document-unique IDs.

Example 2-2. Opening lines of an XForms document

```
<?xml version="1.0"?>
<?xml-stylesheet type="text/css" href="style.css" ?>

<! - the following extremely ugly code is necessary
to make ID attributes behave as expected -->
<!DOCTYPE html [
  <!ATTLIST object id ID #IMPLIED>
  <!ATTLIST model id ID #IMPLIED>
  <!ATTLIST bind id ID #IMPLIED>
  <!ATTLIST instance id ID #IMPLIED>
  <!ATTLIST submission id ID #IMPLIED>
  <!ATTLIST group id ID #IMPLIED>
  <!ATTLIST repeat id ID #IMPLIED>
  <!ATTLIST case id ID #IMPLIED>
]>

<html xmlns="http://www.w3.org/1999/xhtml"
      xmlns:ev="http://www.w3.org/2001/xml-events"
      xmlns:xsi="http://www.w3.org/2001/XMLSchema-instance"
      xmlns:xs="http://www.w3.org/2001/XMLSchema"
      xmlns:u="urn:oasis:names:tc:ubl:CommonAggregateTypes:1.0:0.70"
      xmlns:xforms="http://www.w3.org/2002/xforms">
  <head>
    <title>Create a Purchase Order</title>
```

After the usual XML declaration, the document starts out with a reference to a CSS file to provide style information. Next, the DOCTYPE declaration and the several ATTLIST statements are necessary to make sure that the several ID-typed attributes that will be used are actually treated as IDs.

Following that is the beginning of a normal html element, with several namespace declarations that will be used later in the document. Last is the standard HTML head element, with a title.

The next several lines, in Example 2-3, make up the XForms Model—essentially everything there is to know about the form other than how it will look or otherwise be rendered.

Example 2-3. Starting the XForms Model

```
<xforms:model id="default">
  <!-- schema="schema.xsd" -->
  <xforms:instance src="ubl_samp.xml"/>
  <xforms:submission action="file://tmp/ubl.xml" method="put" id="submit"/>

  <!-- a few things are always required -->
  <xforms:bind nodeset="u:IssueDate" required="true( )" type="xs:date"/>
  <xforms:bind nodeset="u:OrderLine/u:Quantity" required="true( )"
      type="xs:nonNegativeInteger"/>
  <xforms:bind nodeset="u:OrderLine/u:Item/u:BasePrice/u:PriceAmount"
      required="true( )" type="xs:decimal"/>
  <xforms:bind nodeset="u:OrderLine/u:Item/u:SellersItemIdentification/u:ID"
      required="true( )"/>

  <!-- a few basic calculations -->
  <xforms:bind nodeset="u:OrderLine/u:LineExtensionAmount" type="xs:decimal"
      calculate="../u:Quantity * ../u:Item/u:BasePrice/u:PriceAmount"/>
  <xforms:bind nodeset="u:LineExtensionTotalAmount" type="xs:decimal"
      calculate="sum(../u:OrderLine/u:LineExtensionAmount)"/>
```

The xforms:model element is the container for the entire XForms Model. In a document with only one such element, an id attribute isn't strictly needed, though it is good practice to always include one. With the addition of the attribute schema="UBL_Library_0p70_Order.xsd" it would be possible to associate a pre-existing XMLSchema with this form, though that option is commented out here. XML Schema processing would add significant overhead, and the few places that require additional datatype information can be easily specified separately. The xforms:instance element, with the src attribute, points to the initial instance data that was listed earlier. The xforms:submission element indicates that activating submit on this form will write XML to the local file system.

The next several lines contain xforms:bind elements, each of which selects a specific part or parts of the instance data, applying various XForms properties to the selection. The language used to select the XML parts, or *nodes*, is called XPath, which is perhaps better known as the selection language used in XSLT, XPointer, and XML Signature. The next chapter describes XPath in detail. XForms includes defaulting rules that simplify most of the XPath selection expressions, declared on the nodeset attribute, and called *model binding expressions*. The first model binding expression selects the one-and-only u:IssueDate instance data node, marking it as required and of the XML Schema datatype date, which provides the hint that this particular data should be entered with a date-optimized form control, such as a calendar picker. The second model binding expression applies to however many u: Quantity elements happen to exist at any given time, and marks all of them

---

as requiring user entry, along with the XML Schema datatype xs:
nonNegativeInteger.

The next few model binding expressions set up the two calculations that are
fundamental to a purchase order: calculating the total amount for a line item
(price times quantity), and the total for the whole order (sum of all line
items). The calculate attribute holds an XPath expression that gets evaluated to determine a new value for the node to which it is attached. The calculation for line items is ../u:Quantity * ../u:Item/u:BasePrice/u:
PriceAmount, where the asterisk means multiply, and the operands on either
side of it are path expressions, relative to the u:LineExtensionAmount element. In turn, the calculation for the grand total is sum(../u:OrderLine/u:
LineExtensionAmount), which uses the function sum( ) to add up all the values from individual u:LineExtensionAmount nodes. Like a spreadsheet, recal-
culations will occur whenever needed, and dependencies among calculations
will automatically be handled in the correct order. For example, individual
line items will always be multiplied out before the overall total is summed
up.

The definition of the XForms Model continues with the lines in
Example 2-4.

Example 2-4. The rest of the XForms Model

```
<!-- a second instance, temporary data not to be submitted -->
    <xforms:instance id="scratchpad">
      <temp xmlns="">
        <currencyOptions>
          <option value="EUR">Euro</option>
          <option value="GBP">Pound</option>
          <option value="USD">Dollar</option>
        </currencyOptions>
      </temp>
    </xforms:instance>

    <!-- global setting of currencyID -->
    <xforms:bind nodeset="u:OrderLine/u:LineExtensionAmount/@currencyID"
        calculate="../../u:LineExtensionTotalAmount/@currencyID"/>
    <xforms:bind nodeset="u:OrderLine/u:Item/u:BasePrice/u:PriceAmount/
    @currencyID"
        calculate="../../../../u:LineExtensionTotalAmount/@currencyID"/>
  </xforms:model>
</head>
```

An XForms Model can have more than one xforms:instance element. The
usual reason for this is to hold temporary, non-submittable data that is used
in the form. In this example, various currency codes, and the longer descriptions of each, are kept in a separate location for maintainability. This is also

a good example of initial instance data occurring inline in the XForms Model, though it could easily also be another external XML document. The instance data XML itself is not defined in any namespace, so the `xmlns=""` declaration is essential to turn off the default XHTML namespace that would otherwise be in effect at this point.

The last two `xforms:bind` elements set up a mapping across the several `currencyID` attributes that can occur in a UBL document. The form is set up to include a form control that selects the current currency, placing it in the node at `u:LineExtensionTotalAmount/@currencyID`. The two bind elements in this section then copy the value to the appropriate two places in each line item. In theory, each line item could use a different currency type but, for simplicity, this example sets up two calculations that copy the main selection, which is kept on the `u:LineExtensionTotalAmount` element, to every other `currencyID` attribute (the number of which will depend on how many line items are in the order). With this, the XForms Model and the head section of the XHTML document come to a close.

From here on out, the rest of the code is the visible user interface to construct an UBL purchase order. Example 2-5 continues with the definition. Figure 2-2 shows the user interface that results from this portion of the XForms code.

Example 2-5. XForms markup for date, currency type, and total amount

```
<body>
  <xforms:group>
    <xforms:input ref="u:IssueDate">
      <xforms:label>Order Date</xforms:label>
    </xforms:input>

    <xforms:select1 ref="u:LineExtensionTotalAmount/@currencyID"
      appearance="minimal" selection="open">
      <xforms:label>Currency to use throughout this form</xforms:label>
      <xforms:itemset nodeset="instance('scratchpad')/currencyOptions/option">
        <xforms:label ref="."/>
        <xforms:value ref="@value"/>
      </xforms:itemset>
    </xforms:select1>

    <xforms:output ref="u:LineExtensionTotalAmount">
      <xforms:label>Order Total: </xforms:label>
    </xforms:output>
  </xforms:group>
```

The opening of the XHTML body element marks the start of the content that is intended to be rendered. The rest of the content in this section is organized inside an `xforms:group` element. The first form control is a basic input

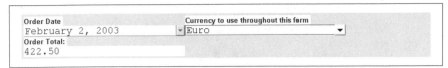

Order Date	Currency to use throughout this form	
February 2, 2003	▾ Euro	▾
Order Total:		
422.50		

Figure 2-2. The user interface rendered for date, currency type, and total amount

control, though due to the XML Schema datatype set up in the XForms Model, most implementations will provide a date-specific entry control, such as a pop-up calendar.

The second form control is a single select control, with a hint attribute appearance="minimal" to suggest that this part of the interface should be given minimal screen estate when not activated—in other words, a pop-up list. Another attribute selection="open" indicates that the user should be able to enter arbitrary values not on the list, in which case the entered value would have to be a three-letter currency code, not the friendlier text description that comes with the built-in choices. The xforms:itemset element pulls the choices from the instance data, in this case from the secondary instance data, as can be seen by the instance( ) function in the XPath, which is needed any time the non-default instance data is referenced. A kind of repetition is going on here; despite the single xforms:itemset element, the list will have one choice for each node matched in the secondary instance data.

The output control displays data but doesn't provide any interface for changing it.

Example 2-6 is lengthier, but not difficult to understand.

Example 2-6. XForms markup for addresses

```
<xforms:switch id="DetailHider">
  <xforms:case id="detail_hide">
    <xforms:trigger>
      <xforms:label>Show Details</xforms:label>
      <xforms:toggle ev:event="DOMActivate" case="detail_show"/>
    </xforms:trigger>
  </xforms:case>

  <xforms:case id="detail_show">
    <xforms:group id="SellerParty" ref="u:SellerParty">
      <xforms:label>Seller Information:</xforms:label>
      <xforms:input ref="u:PartyName/u:Name">
        <xforms:label>Name</xforms:label>
      </xforms:input>
      <xforms:group ref="u:Address">
        <xforms:input ref="u:Street">
          <xforms:label>Street</xforms:label>
        </xforms:input>
        <xforms:input ref="u:CityName">
```

Example 2-6. XForms markup for addresses (continued)

```
            <xforms:label>City</xforms:label>
          </xforms:input>
          <xforms:input ref="u:PostalZone">
            <xforms:label>Postal Code</xforms:label>
          </xforms:input>
          <xforms:input ref="u:CountrySub-Entity">
            <xforms:label>State or Province</xforms:label>
          </xforms:input>
        </xforms:group>
      </xforms:group>

      <xforms:group id="BuyerParty" ref="u:BuyerParty">
        <xforms:label>Buyer Information:</xforms:label>
        <xforms:input ref="u:PartyName/u:Name">
          <xforms:label>Name</xforms:label>
        </xforms:input>
        <xforms:group ref="u:Address">
          <xforms:input ref="u:Street">
            <xforms:label>Street</xforms:label>
          </xforms:input>
          <xforms:input ref="u:CityName">
            <xforms:label>City</xforms:label>
          </xforms:input>
          <xforms:input ref="u:PostalZone">
            <xforms:label>Postal Code</xforms:label>
          </xforms:input>
          <xforms:input ref="u:CountrySub-Entity">
            <xforms:label>State or Province</xforms:label>
          </xforms:input>
        </xforms:group>
      </xforms:group>

      <xforms:trigger>
        <xforms:label>Hide Details</xforms:label>
        <xforms:toggle ev:event="DOMActivate" case="detail_hide"/>
      </xforms:trigger>
    </xforms:case>
</xforms:switch>
```

Figure 2-3 shows the initial state of the user interface produced by this portion of the XForms code. Figure 2-4 shows the result of toggling the switch, revealing the form controls for entering the buyer and seller information.

Figure 2-3. The user interface for the XForms switch element, collapsed

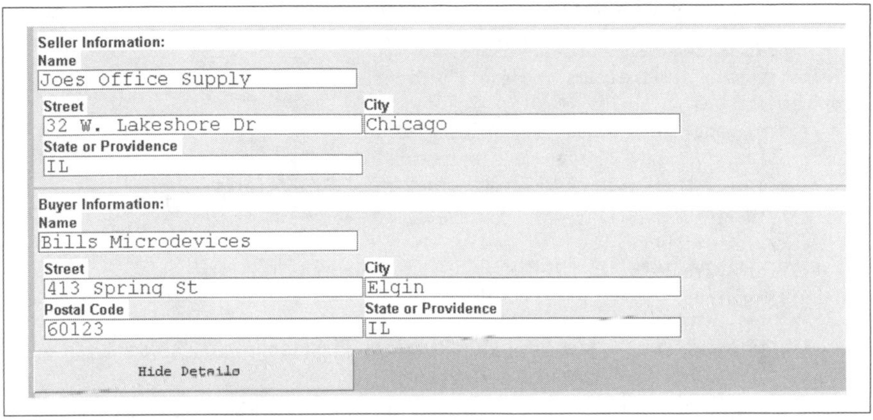

Figure 2-4. The user interface for the XForms switch element, expanded

The xforms:switch element is a useful tool to show different portions of the user interface on command. In this case, the form controls for seller and buyer information are either entirely shown or entirely hidden. A declarative element, xforms:toggle, changes which of the xforms:case elements get to have its contents rendered, with all others suppressed. The first case, which is the default, displays only an xforms:trigger that toggles itself away, showing all the form controls in the next case in its place.

Within another group for organizational purposes, the form controls in the next section capture all the information needed about the seller referenced by the purchase order. In this case, the overall group has a label, in addition to labels on the individual form controls.

The next group, for the buyer information, is nearly identical to the one that precedes it. While earlier drafts of XForms had a technique to combine this duplicated code in a single place, that feature was dropped in favor of concentrating on getting the underlying framework correct. (One proposal involves combining XSLT with XForms, using the element template to define a template that can be instantiated multiple times throughout the document.)

The last part of this section is another xforms:toggle displayed along with the buyer and shipper information. Upon activation, it causes the contents of the first case to be displayed, which has the effect of hiding all the buyer and shipper interface. The XML instance data, however, continues to exist even when the means of viewing or changing are hidden from view.

Example 2-7 creates a dynamically expandable list of line items.

Example 2-7. Using XForms to create an expandable list.

```
<!-- repeating sequence for line items -->
<xforms:repeat id="lineitems" nodeset="u:OrderLine">
  <xforms:group>
    <xforms:range ref="u:Quantity" class="narrow"
        start="1" end="9" step="1" incremental="true">
      <xforms:label>Quantity <xforms:output ref="."/></xforms:label>
    </xforms:range>

    <xforms:input ref="u:Item/u:Description" class="wide">
      <xforms:label>Description</xforms:label>
    </xforms:input>
    <xforms:input ref="u:Item/u:SellersItemIdentification/u:ID" class="wide">
      <xforms:label>Part Number</xforms:label>
    </xforms:input>
    <xforms:input ref="u:Item/u:BasePrice/u:PriceAmount" class="narrow">
      <xforms:label>Price</xforms:label>
    </xforms:input>
  </xforms:group>
</xforms:repeat>

<xforms:group id="RepeatDashboard">
  <xforms:trigger>
    <xforms:label>Insert new line</xforms:label>
    <xforms:insert ev:event="DOMActivate" position="after"
      nodeset="u:OrderLine" at="index('lineitems')"/>
  </xforms:trigger>

  <xforms:trigger>
    <xforms:label>Remove current line</xforms:label>
    <xforms:delete ev:event="DOMActivate" nodeset="u:OrderLine"
      at="index('lineitems')"/>
  </xforms:trigger>
</xforms:group>
```

Figure 2-5 shows the user interface that results from this portion of the XForms code, with the first line item highlighted.

Like xforms:itemset seen earlier, xforms:repeat causes a repetition of content, once for each node in a given set of nodes—exactly the behavior needed to populate the u:OrderLine elements from UBL. All the content of xforms:repeat is effectively duplicated as many times as there are line items, which can be dynamically added and removed. The first form control on each line item is xforms:range, which allows a smoother way to select a value than typing a number; for example, a sliding indicator. The range here is from 1 to 9.

The rest of the repeating form controls are similar to ones already used in this example. One difference is the class attribute on the final xforms:input, which is used by the associated CSS to style the form control.

Quantity 5								Description
ı	ı	ı	ı	ı	ı	ı	ı	Pencils, box #2 red
Part Number								Price
32145-12								2.50
Quantity 12								Description
ı	ı	ı	ı	ı	ı	ı	ı	Xeorox Paper- case
Part Number								Price
78-697-24								30.00
Quantity 10								Description
ı	ı	ı	ı	ı	ı	ı	ı	Pens, box, blue finepoint
Part Number								Price
091356-3								5.00
Insert new line				Remove current line				

Figure 2-5. The user interface for repeating line items

Outside of the repeat, a few interesting things are happening. Inside another group, an xforms:trigger is configured to insert a new line item. Another declarative action, xforms:insert, accomplishes this feat. The location of the inserted line item is either just before or just after a specific location (from the at attribute) within a particular node-set (from the nodeset attribute).

The xforms:delete action works similarly. Any repeating set keeps track of the currently active item, called the *index*. Both the insert and delete actions make use of the index, as obtained through the index( ) function.

The concluding part of the sample document, in Example 2-8, allows the completed document to be written to disk.

Example 2-8. XForms markup to submit the data

```
<xforms:submit submission="submit">
    <xforms:label>Write to disk</xforms:label>
  </xforms:submit>
 </body>
</html>
```

Figure 2-6 shows the rendering for this piece of XForms code.

Figure 2-6. The user interface to finalize the purchase order

The xforms:submit element is another form control, like xforms:trigger, but able to invoke the submission procedure without any additional coding needed. It contains a reference to the xforms:submission element contained in the XForms Model, which ultimately determines what happens when this control is activated. After the last form control, the XHTML document comes to its usual conclusion.

Host Language Issues

The philosophy of the XForms specification can be summed up in a single line, found in the Abstract of the official W3C XForms document.

> XForms is not a free-standing document type, but is intended to be integrated into other markup languages, such as XHTML or SVG.

This approach has benefits as well as drawbacks. The benefits are that the XForms specification was completed more quickly, and without host language dependencies that otherwise might exist. The primary disadvantage is that more work needs to be done to actually integrate XForms with XHTML, SVG, or any other language.

Another W3C specification, *Modularization of XHTML*, provides a framework in which XHTML, or any other combination of XML-based languages, can be mixed and matched in order to provide a combined document type. Such combinations can take advantage of specific language features; for example, in XHTML a non-rendered head section can contain the XForms Model, and in SVG, a `foreignObject` element can enclose individual form controls.

Combined Document Types

Any document that uses XForms will necessarily be a combined document type, involving multiple XML namespaces. Such compound documents are still largely uncharted territory in the realm of W3C specifications, which leads to several headaches. For one thing, XML has the concept of attributes of type ID, specifying a document-unique value. Unfortunately, the *id-ness* of the attribute needs to be declared in a DTD or some kind of schema, which can only occur at the top of the overall document, not at the point where a subdocument starts. DTDs in general are poorly suited to validation, so until further work is done within the W3C, some XForms documents will have to suffice with being simply well-formed.

Although often scorned by developers, XML namespaces are a fact of life, particularly for W3C specifications. XForms elements conforming to the final W3C Recommendation are defined in a namespace of *http://www.w3.org/2002/xforms*. Other specifications could, in theory, include all the XForms elements in their own namespace, though this seems unlikely for official W3C specifications. Examples in this book show a mixture of both approaches.

One glimmer of hope is a recurring proposal for an attribute named `xml:id`, which would be recognized as having *id-ness* without a separate DTD or Schema. In examples throughout this book, any attributes named `id` will be considered to have been appropriately declared to be unique identifiers.

In a similar category is an attribute usually named `class`, which serves as a hook for attaching style sheets. As used throughout this chapter, the host language is responsible for defining this attribute and attaching it to the XForms elements.

Linking Attributes

Another attribute, `src`, has caused nearly as much controversy as its big brother in XHTML, `href`. The problem stems from tension with XLink 1.0, a W3C Recommendation, which asserts itself as the preferred technique to define any "explicit relationship between resources or portions of resources." Originally, this standard was envisioned by some as a solution that could apply to any XML, but the final solution worked only with an attribute named `xlink:href` (complete with a separate namespace).

The inflexibility of XLink causes problems in modularized documents, including XForms, since there are different kinds of links but only one allowed attribute name. As an example, an element might both serve as a launching point for a hyperlink, and at the same time link to external inline content, as in the following fragment that might result from a combination of XForms and SVG (which uses `xlink:href`):

```
<xforms:label src="label2.svg" xlink:href="homepage.html"/>
```

In this example, the `src` attribute from XForms points to a SVG file to be used as the label, and the `xlink:href` attribute from SVG makes the label a clickable hyperlink to *homepage.html*. It's a good thing that the XForms attribute is named `src` and not `xlink:href`, because a conflict would have resulted when trying to combine the languages, since an element can't have two attributes with the same name.

As an alternative to XLink, the HTML Working Group proposed another standard, called HLink, to annotate any XML with link descriptions. The proposal met with almost as little enthusiasm as XLink. The Technical Architecture Group (TAG) of the W3C is looking into the issue; the long term resolution remains to be seen. Controversies aside, in XForms, src consistently means one thing: that the URI in the attribute value is to be fetched as part of loading the document, and the contents rendered in place of whatever element contains the attribute (much like the img element in earlier versions of XHTML).

CHAPTER 3

XPath in XForms

*"Nobody trips over mountains. It is the small
pebble that causes you to stumble. Pass all the
pebbles in your path and you will find you have
crossed the mountain."*

—*Traditional proverb*

The most obvious difference between XForms and earlier technologies is the
representation of form data as XML instead of flat name/value pairs. While
a richer data representation was a welcome change, it also called for a more
sophisticated language to reference structured data. The W3C had already
defined just such a language, called XPath (*http://www.w3.org/TR/xpath*), a
component of XSLT (*http://www.w3.org/TR/xslt*), an XML vocabulary used
for transforming one flavor of XML into another. The XPath specification
was built with the intention that later specifications could use it as a foundation, which is exactly what XForms does. This chapter first lays out the
foundation of XPath, and then shows how XForms builds on that foundation.

What exactly is XPath? The "path" portion of the name comes from the similar appearance of many XPath expressions to directory paths in a filesystem, as shown in Example 3-1. XPath also includes some lightweight
calculation functionality, such as basic mathematics, rounding, and string
manipulation, which the calculation engine in XForms takes advantage of
instead of defining a new (and incompatible) language.

Example 3-1. Some XPath expressions

```
/html/head/title
html:head/xforms:model/@xml:id
../items
purchaseOrder/items/item[3]
purchaseOrder/items/item[@price = 12.34]
```

Example 3-1. Some XPath expressions (continued)

```
string-length('hello world')
purchaseOrder/subtotal * instance('taxtable')/tax
total * instance('taxtable')/rate
```

Each of these examples demonstrates a particular aspect of how XPath is used for addressing parts of an XML document. But must the XML always exist as a distinct document? No. The data structure addressed by XPath is carefully defined—by the XPath Data Model. Detailed knowledge of the data model isn't required to start using XPath, though. A few basic concepts are all that is needed to begin.

Getting Up to Speed with XPath

The remainder of this chapter after this section serves as a detailed XPath reference. In many cases, however, only a basic level of XPath is needed in XForms. (Chapter 10 shows one common design pattern for forms that requires virtually no special XPath knowledge.) If you are new to XPath, this section will provide the necessary background that will enable you to read and write simple XPath expressions with confidence.

Simple XPath expressions resemble file system paths, except that instead of navigating across directories and files, XPath expressions navigate across XML *nodes*—the XPath term for any individual piece of XML such as an element, attribute, or piece of text. For example, the expression:

```
/html/head/title
```

represents an absolute path through XML, starting at a special root node, then progressing through child elements html, head, and title. The XML referenced by this path might look something like this:

```
<html>
  <head>
    <title>Push Button Paradise</title>
  ...
```

Since XML names can be qualified with a namespace, it's also possible to use colonized names at any step. Relative paths are also possible, in which case it's important to know what the *context node* (similar in concept to the current directory) is. Additionally, attributes can be addressed with a leading @ character, leading to XPath expressions like this:

```
html:head/xforms:model/@id
```

Note that when the leading slash is omitted, the path expression is relative.

Path expressions can be said to return a *node-set*. Both of the above examples conveniently returned a node-set consisting of a single node, but in the general case, node-sets can have zero, one, or a multitude of nodes. XForms includes a *first node rule*, that in certain circumstances, will reduce a larger node-set down to a single node, namely, the first one according to the order the elements appear in the document. Also, node-sets can be filtered manually using a *predicate*. Predicates are identified using square brackets as follows:

```
purchaseOrder/items/item[3]
```

This expression is processed by first selecting all item nodes that are children of an items node (which, in turn, must be a child of a purchaseOrder node, which, in turn, must be a child of the context node...whew!). The resulting node-set is then filtered to include only the third node, in the order that the elements appear in the document. If there is no third item node, then the result will be an empty node-set, not any kind of an error condition.

> The predicate can contain any kind of test that yields a Boolean (true/false) answer, including greater-than and less-than tests. The literal characters < and >, however, aren't generally safe to use in XML, and should be escaped as < and > respectively. An expression using this kind of test might look like this: item[@price < 12.34].

XPath expressions can also be more than just paths, and can be thought of as a kind of lightweight scripting language. Besides node-sets, an expression can evaluate to a Boolean value, a string, or a number. For example, the expression:

```
string-length('hello world')
```

would always return 11 as a number, and the expression:

```
purchaseOrder/subtotal * instance('taxtable')/tax
```

represents a full-blown calculation that might appear in a real-world form. On the right-hand side of the multiplication symbol, note that the path expression begins with a function call that can return a node-set from another location (a different XForms instance, in this case).

Going Deep: The XPath Data Model

In the XPath view of things, elements, attributes, text, comments, processing instructions, and even namespaces are represented internally as nodes connected in a tree shape. Some nodes, such as elements, may have child nodes, while others, such as attributes, have no children, as restricted by XML rules. A special node, called the root node, serves as the ultimate ancestor node.

XML Information Set Mapping

XPath 1.0 was completed in November 1999 with a section outlining the XPath Data Model and an appendix defining the mapping to the then-unfinished W3C specification called *XML Information Set* or "infoset" for short. This formalized description of the XML Data Model, available at *http://www. w3.org/TR/xml-infoset/*, was completed in October 2001. Subsequently, an errata to XPath, at *http://www.w3.org/1999/11/REC-xpath-19991116-errata/*, finalized the infoset mapping.

Example 3-2 shows a short XML document, and Figure 3-1 shows how that document would be represented by a tree of nodes.

In this example, note that neither the XML declaration nor the DOCTYPE declaration produce any nodes. Thus, these XML data structures are effectively invisible to XPath and, by extension, XForms. On the other hand, notice how each element node has two namespace nodes attached: one for the xmlns:html declaration on the root element, which applies throughout, and one for the built-in declaration of the xml prefix, as seen in the attribute xml: lang. Even a short document like this generates a huge number of nodes!

Example 3-2. A basic XML document, represented as text

```
<!DOCTYPE html PUBLIC "-//W3C//DTD XHTML 1.1//EN"
    "http://www.w3.org/TR/xhtml11/DTD/xhtml11.dtd">
<?xml-stylesheet href="screen.css" type="text/css" media="screen"?>
<html xmlns="http://www.w3.org/1999/xhtml" xml:lang="en">
  <head>
    <title>Virtual Library</title>
  </head>
  <body>
    <p>Moved to <a href="http://vlib.example.org/">vlib.example.org</a>.</p>
  </body>
</html>
```

Each node has a set of properties that are exposed to XPath in various ways.

- A name. Some nodes, like the root node, comments, and text nodes will always have a name of the empty string (""). Elements and attributes have an expanded name, a combination of a local name plus a namespace URI. Processing instructions use their target, which is not

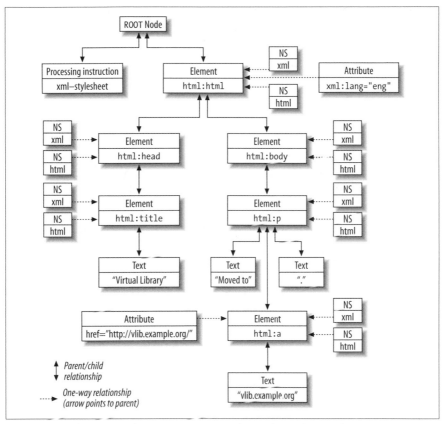

Figure 3-1. A basic XML document, represented as nodes in the XPath data model

subject to namespace processing, as a name. Namespace nodes have the namespace prefix as a name.

- A string value. Text nodes contain the text characters from the source XML, with line endings normalized to #xA as required by the XML specification. Text nodes will always contain as much text as possible, and, thus, no two consecutive children will ever both be text nodes and the location of CDATA sections is not preserved. Comment nodes contain the full text of the comment (minus the `<!--` and `-->` delimiters). Attributes contain the attribute value, and processing instructions contain the text after the initial target and whitespace, and up to and not including the terminating `?>`. Namespace nodes contain a URI (or the empty string) as a name. The root node and element nodes compute their string value by recursively concatenating the string values of all descendant nodes.

- Children. In theory, you can ask about children of any node, but only the root node and element nodes will actually have children.
- A position relative to all other nodes. The overall ordering is called the document order.

Additionally, some nodes have the following properties:

- A parent. Every node but the special root node has exactly one parent.
- Attributes. Elements may also contain attributes, which are treated specially and not considered children.
- Namespaces. Namespace nodes are also treated specially, and are not considered to have a child relationship with the element node to which they attach.

A collection of nodes without duplicates is referred to as a node-set.

Location Paths

A key requirement for dissecting nearly any XPath expression is an understanding of *Location Paths*, which select one or more nodes based on their location or other properties. A Location Path consists of a number of individual Location Steps, each separated by a slash (/). Each individual step builds upon the previous steps to traverse the document, and can be a test against the name of a node, or one of the following special tests:

node( )
: Matches any node whatsoever.

text( )
: Matches any text node.

comment( )
: Matches any comment node.

processing-instruction( )
: Matches any processing instruction node, and may have a parameter to match against a specific processing instruction.

Another special test is *, which will match any element node (or attribute node within the attribute axis, or namespace node within the namespace axis.) Similarly, another special test *prefix*:* will match any node identified with the namespace mapped to *prefix*.

Figure 3-2 illustrates how a path is traversed in steps, from left to right.

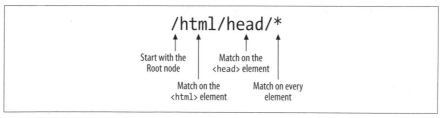

Figure 3-2. Location paths and steps

 Extra care is needed when traversing a document that contains XML namespaces, especially with defaulted namespaces. Any namespace prefixes in scope can be used in Location Steps; however, *default namespaces in scope do not apply to the XPath expression.*

For example, to address the item elements in this example:

```
<purchaseOrder xmlns="http://po.example.org">
    <items>
        <item/>
        <item/>
        <item/>
    </items>
</purchaseOrder>
```

The prefixes used in the XPath expression are not required to match the prefixes used in the XML being addressed, since only the combination of local name plus namespace URI matters. Because of the way XPath treats (or doesn't treat, actually) default namespaces, the namespace http://po.example.org needs to be mapped to a specific prefix, regardless of any default namespace in scope at the point of the XPath expression. XForms markup to accomplish this might look like this:

```
<xforms:bind nodeset="po:purchaseOrder/po:items/po:
item" xmlns:po="http://po.example.org"/>
```

In summary: every namespace referenced in an XPath expression needs to be associated with a specific prefix at the point where the XPath expression occurs.

Context

Just as a relative directory path is relative to a current directory, XPath expressions are evaluated relative to a "context," which consists of the following:

- A context node
- A pair of non-zero positive integers (the context position and the context size)

- Variable bindings (not used in XForms)
- A function library
- The set of namespace declarations in scope for the expression

 Remember, one thing in XPath that is *not* part of the context is a default namespace. The developing XPath 2.0, however, promises to change this.

An XPath expression of . selects the context node, and .. selects the parent node of the context node. Any expression that begins with / is an absolute path and independent from the context node. Other, more complicated, paths through the Data Model are possible, since there are many possible ways or axes in which to navigate through XML.

Axes

Each Location Step includes an axis, which is an instruction on how to navigate the tree structure. Since XPath is a general-purpose language, there are many axes that don't make much sense for XForms, but Table 3-1 summarizes all of them for completeness.

Table 3-1. XPath axes

Axis name	Description
child	Contains the children of the context node. (As a consequence, this axis never contains attribute or namespace nodes.)
attribute	Contains the attributes of the context node. (As a consequence, this axis is always empty, unless the context node is an element.)
parent	Contains the parent of the context node. (As a consequence, this axis is always empty when the context node is the root node.)
descendant	Contains the descendants of the context node; a descendant is a child or a child of a child and so on. (As a consequence, this axis never contains attribute or namespace nodes.)
descendant-or-self	Contains the context node and the descendants of the context node. (As a consequence, this axis never contains attribute or namespace nodes.)
ancestor	Contains the ancestors of the context node; the ancestors of the context node consist of the parent of context node and the parent's parent and so on. (As a consequence, this axis always includes the root node, unless the context node itself is the root node.)
ancestor-or-self	Contains the context node and the ancestors of the context node. (As a consequence, this axis always includes the root node.)

Table 3-1. XPath axes (continued)

Axis name	Description
following	Contains all nodes in the same document as the context node that are after the context node in document order, excluding any descendants and excluding attribute nodes and namespace nodes.
following-sibling	Contains all the following siblings of the context node. (As a consequence, this axis is always empty when the context node is an attribute node or a namespace node.)
preceding	Contains all nodes in the same document as the context node that are before the context node in document order, excluding any ancestors and excluding attribute nodes and namespace nodes.
preceding-sibling	Contains all the preceding siblings of the context node. (As a consequence, this axis is always empty when the context node is an attribute node or a namespace node.)
namespace	Contains the namespace nodes of the context node. (As a consequence, this axis is always empty unless the context node is an element.)
self	Contains just the context node itself.

Abbreviated axes

As earlier examples have shown, the default axis is child, so a/b is the same as child::a/child::b.

Another convenient shortcut is that attribute:: can be replaced by @, so @id is the same as attribute::id.

A few more useful abbreviations are . for self::node( ); .. for parent:: node( ); and // for /descendant-or-self::node( )/. This last abbreviation is useful when you want to select every element by a certain name, regardless of where it appears in the tree. For example, //p selects every p element no matter where it occurs.

Predicates

A bare Location Path expression selects every node that matches the path it specifies. For example, the expression html/body/p selects every p element that's a direct child of body. Often, it is desirable to filter down the selection even more. In XPath, this is done through a predicate, which appears in square brackets and can apply to any Location Step in a Location Path. To select only the first p from the earlier example, the expression would be /html/body/p[position( )=1], or, even shorter, /html/body/p[1].

The predicate expression evaluates to a true or false result (or a number that is special-cased as a comparison against position( )). The way this works is:

1. A new context is created with the node it is attached to as the context node. The number of nodes in the node-set at that point is the context size.

   For each node, a new context is created with the node it is attached to as the context node, with the number of nodes in the node-set at that point as the context size, and with the context position being the position of the node within the node-set. For axes that go "backwards," namely ancestor, ancestor-or-self, preceding, and preceding-sibling, the position counter is mirrored so that, for instance, ancestor:: element[2] would select the 2nd ancestor element as expected.

2. If the expression evaluates to true, the node is included in the filtered node-set.

Multiple predicates can be specified on any given step, which will result in multiple layers of filtering on the node-set. If a node-set gets filtered down to nothing, no error results—the expression simply returns an empty node-set. Figure 3-3 illustrates how filtering works through predicates.

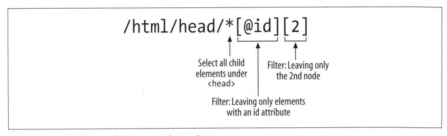

Figure 3-3. Node-set filtering with predicates

Computed Expressions

The preceding section discussed how addressing works in XPath. The language is also capable of performing simple computations that return strings, booleans, or numbers. XForms defines the term *Computed Expression* to represent this special usage of XPath.

Datatypes in XPath and XForms

The term *datatype* can get a little confusing during discussions on XForms, since both XPath and XML Schema contain the notion of a datatype—and the two don't always agree on the details.

XPath expressions have four major datatypes: node-sets, strings, booleans, and numbers. (Note that only the expressions contain the notion of datatypes, and the Data Model itself is datatype free, although early drafts of XPath 2.0 appear to change this) Of these, string and boolean are similar to the XML Schema datatypes of the same name, although XML Schema booleans differ in that they allow both "1" and "true" for true, and "0" and "false" for false. Because of this, hacky workarounds are sometimes needed, as described later. The number datatype in XPath represents a double-precision floating point number under the rules defined by the IEEE (which includes positive and negative infinity, positive and negative zero, and a special 'not a number' value), and is thus comparable with the XML Schema datatype double. Node-sets do not have a convenient analog in XML Schema.

One other convention you might run into in the XPath specification is a datatype called "object", which simply means 'any datatype'. The XPath function descriptions below use this same convention.

It's unusual to run into type conflicts in XPath, mainly because the flexible type conversion rules, which are defined below as the functions string( ), number( ), and boolean( ), tend to stay out of your way. In short, nearly any time a specific datatype is expected, a different datatype will get automatically converted into the expected datatype. For example, the expression "a/b * a/c" might seem to multiply two node-sets, at first glance. This works as expected, however, since the multiplication operator first converts each node-set into a number, then multiplies to arrive at a result (just as if the expression had been "number(a/b) * number(a/c)"). Operators and function parameters in XPath behave this way, which avoids a lot of pain for those who need to write XPath expressions.

Operators

Arithmetic basics (+, -, *, div, and mod)

XPath includes all the arithmetic basics: plus, minus, multiply, divide, modulus, and unary minus (which negates the single operand). All of these operators convert their operands into numbers if needed, as with a call to number( ).

Order of Precedence

Any time an expression uses more than one operator, it is necessary to know what precedence is used. For XPath, this is (lowest to highest, with semicolons as separators where necessary):

1. or
2. and
3. =; !=
4. <=; <; >=; >
5. +; -
6. *; div; mod; unary -
7. | (union)

Operators at the same precedence level are always evaluated left-to-right. Parentheses can be used to force the expression to evaluate in a different order than the default.

Equality comparisons (=and !=)

Comparing whether one thing is the same as another or not is straightforward, though some of the type combinations get interesting.

When comparing two node-sets, the comparison looks at the individual nodes. If *any* node in the left-hand node-set has a string-value that meets the equals or not-equals comparison with the string-value of *any* node in the right-hand node-set, the overall comparison succeeds. Similarly, if one side is a node-set and the other side is either a string or a number, the comparison will succeed if any node in the node-set meets the comparison. In comparing a boolean and any other datatype, the other datatype is converted as with a call to boolean( ) before comparison. Otherwise, if at least one object to be compared is a number, then the other object is converted as with a call to number( ) before comparison. Finally, comparisons between the same datatypes for strings, numbers, and booleans can be done directly.

Relational comparisons (<, >, <=, and =>)

The rules for relational comparisons follow the same rules as above when at least one operand is a node-set. In all other cases, both operands are converted if necessary into a number, as with a call to number( ) before comparison.

Boolean operations (or, and)

Boolean expressions can be connected together with logical or and and operators. (Note that not( ) is available also, but as a function, not an operator)

Node-set unions (|)

A final operator performs a union operation on a node-set. Note that the resulting node-set (like all node-sets) will contain no duplicate nodes.

Functions

XPath defines a number of built-in functions, and XForms adds a few more. This section lists every built-in function. Note that even though function parameters are unnamed in XPath, the descriptions below include parameter names for descriptive purposes.

---

position( )   returns the context position from the expression evaluation

Parameters: \<none>   **Defined in:** XPath 1.0
Return type: number

This example returns the 4th para element child of the context node (or an empty node-set if there is no 4th para element):

```
para[position()=4]
```

---

last( )   returns the context size from the expression evaluation context

Parameters: \<none>   **Defined in:** XPath 1.0
Return type: number

This example returns the last para element child of the context node:

```
para[position()=last()]
```

---

count( )   returns the number of nodes in a node-set

Parameters: node-set ns (required)   **Defined in:** XPath 1.0
Return type: number

This example returns the number of item elements that are children of the items element:

```
count( items/item )
```

---

id( )

Parameters: object obj (required)   **Defined in:** XPath 1.0
Return type: node-set

Normally, this function is used to return the single node with an ID that matches
the string value passed in as a parameter. When a space-separated list or a node-
set is passed in, it will return the union of all nodes that individually match the
IDs. This function normally appears on the left-hand side of a path expression.

Determining what is a 'unique' ID is harder than it looks.

The XPath 1.0 Recommendation states that "If a document
does not have a DTD, then no element in the document will
have a unique ID." In XForms, a DTD will never be associated with instance data. An XML Schema, however, has a
datatype called xs:ID, which can be associated with an
instance data node to provide an indication that the node
contains a unique id. Thus, it is still possible for the id( )
function to be useful in XForms, though it takes a little extra
work.

This example selects the element with the unique ID "taxtable" (if any) and
returns a node-set of all the rate element children:

```
id("taxtable")/rate
```

local-name( )

returns the local part of the name of a node,
without regard to any XML namespace

Parameters: node-set ns (optional)   **Defined in:** XPath 1.0
Return type: string

Only the first node (in document order) of the node-set is considered. When
called with no parameters, the local name of the context node is returned.

This example returns the local name of the element xforms:model, which is
"model":

```
local-name(xforms:model)
```

namespace-uri( )

returns the namespace URI of a the name of a node,
without regard to the local name

Parameters: node-set ns (optional)   **Defined in:** XPath 1.0
Return type: string

Only the first node (in document order) of the node-set is considered. For
anything other than attribute and element nodes, the return value will always be

the empty string. When called with no parameters, the namespace URI of the context node is returned.

This example returns the namespace URI of the element xforms:model, which is http://www.w3.org/2002/xforms:

```
namespace-uri(xforms:model)
```

---

name( )   for element and attribute nodes, returns the node name as a QName

Parameters: node-set ns (optional)   **Defined in:** XPath 1.0
Return type: string

For other node types, returns the same value as local-name( ). When called with no parameters, the name of the context node is returned.

This example returns the QName of the element xforms:model, which is "xforms: model":

```
name(xforms:model)
```

---

string( )   converts another datatype into a string

Parameters: object str (optional)   **Defined in:** XPath 1.0
Return type: string

Conversion from other datatypes proceeds according to the following rules:

node-set
> The string-value of the node-set (which is the concatenation of the string-value of all descendant nodes) is returned.

number
> A string representing the number is returned, or one of the special values of Infinity, -Infinity, or NaN (short for not a number).

boolean
> Either true or false is returned.

When called with no parameters, the converted value of the context node is returned.

This example returns a string equal to the string-value of the title element, which in HTML would be a single text node:

```
string(/html/head/title)
```

concat( )

returns the concatenation of all the string parameters

Parameters: string s1 (required); string s2 (required); any number of additional optional strings

Defined in: XPath 1.0

Return type: string

The example combines all four string parameters into a single string, "Hello World!":

```
concat( 'Hello', ' ', 'World', '!')
```

starts-with( )

returns true if the src string starts with the substr string

Parameters: string src (required); string substr (required)

Defined in: XPath 1.0

Return type: boolean

This example returns true:

```
starts-with('Hello World!', 'H')
```

contains( )

returns true if the src string contains the substr string

Parameters: string src (required); string substr (required)

Defined in: XPath 1.0

Return type: boolean

This example returns true:

```
contains('Hello World!', 'r')
```

substring-before( )

returns the portion of the src occurring before the substr string

Parameters: string src (required); string substr (required)

Defined in: XPath 1.0

Return type: string

If the substr string is found within the larger string, this function returns the portion of the src string up to and not including the first matched substr. If not found, returns the empty string.

This example returns the string "1999":

```
substring-before("1999-04-01","-")
```

substring-after( )

returns the portion of the src occurring after the substr string

Parameters: string src (required); string substr (required)

Defined in: XPath 1.0

Return type: string

If the substr string is found within the larger string, this function returns the portion of the src string after and not including the first matched substr string. If not found, returns the empty string.

This example returns the string "04-01":

```
substring-after("1999-04-01","-")
```

substring( )

returns a selected substring of the src string

Parameters: string src (required); number start (required);   **Defined in:** XPath 1.0
number length (optional)

Return type: string

The returned substring is determined by starting with the startth character, and continuing on for length characters. If the length parameter is omitted, the returned string continues on to the end of the src string.

The following example returns "34", and the second following example returns "345":

```
substring("12345", 3, 2)
substring("12345", 3)
```

string-length( )

returns the number of characters in the src string

Parameters: string src (optional)   **Defined in:** XPath 1.0

Return type: number

When called with no parameters, returns the number of characters in the context node converted to a string.

This example returns 12:

```
string-length("Hello World!")
```

normalize-space( )

returns the src with certain whitespace characters collapsed

Parameters: string src (optional)   **Defined in:** XPath 1.0

Return type: string

This function removes all leading and trailing whitespace, and all other consecutive whitespace characters are replaced with a single space. When called with no parameters, returns the normalized value of the context node converted to a string.

This example returns "Hello World!":

```
normalize-space("  Hello    World!    ")
```

translate( )

returns the src string, with characters replaced from a list

Parameters: string src (required), string removechars   **Defined in:** XPath 1.0
(required), string replacechars (required)

Return type: string

Characters from the removechars string replaced with characters from the corresponding position in the replacechars string. The removechars string may be longer than the replacechars string, in which case the additional characters are simply removed from the src string.

In many languages, translate( ) can be used to perform case conversion. For example, to convert English to uppercase, the call you need would be translate(*src*, "abcdefghijklmnopqrstuvwxyz", "ABCDEFGHIJKLMNOPQRSTUVWXYZ").

A future edition of XPath may include specific functions for case conversion.

The first example returns "hello world!", and the second example returns "hello world" (note that the exclamation point is gone):

```
translate("Hello World!", "HW", "hw")
translate("Hello World!", "HW!", "hw")
```

---

boolean( ) converts another datatype into a boolean

Parameters: object bool (optional)   **Defined in:** XPath 1.0
Return type: boolean

Other datatypes are converted according to the following rules:

node-set
    An empty node-set produces false; anything else produces true.

number
    Zero and NaN produce false; anything else produces true.

string
    An empty string produces false; anything else produces true.

When called with no parameters, the converted value of the context node is returned.

This example returns true if the Location Path a/b happens to select one or more nodes; otherwise, it returns false:

```
boolean(a/b)
```

---

not( ) returns the logical negation of the argument

Parameters: boolean b (required)   **Defined in:** XPath 1.0
Return type: boolean

This example returns false if the Location Path a/b happens to select one or more nodes; otherwise, it returns true:

```
not(a/b)
```

true( )

Parameters: none
Return type: boolean

Defined in: XPath 1.0

This example returns true:

```
true( )
```

false( )

Parameters: none
Return type: boolean

Defined in: XPath 1.0

This example returns false:

```
false( )
```

lang( )

checks the language of the context node

Parameters: string langcode (required)
Return type: boolean

Defined in: XPath 1.0

This function examines the context node and returns true if the declared language (with an xml:lang attribute) matches. The comparison takes into account the rules for language identifiers, such that a search for "en" will still match "en-gb". If the context node doesn't contain an xml:lang attribute, the nearest ancestor element node with an xml:lang attribute will be consulted. If no xml:lang declaration can be located, the return value is false.

For an XPath data model matching the following XML:

```
<root xml:lang="x-klingon">
  <context/>
</root>
```

With context as the context node, this example returns true:

```
lang("x")
```

number( )

converts another datatype into a number

Parameters: object num (required)
Return type: number

Defined in: XPath 1.0

Other datatypes are converted according to the following rules:

string
> A string that represents a number (ignoring leading and trailing whitespace) is converted into a number. Any string that can't be converted this way results in a return value of NaN.

boolean

true produces 1 and false produces 0.

node-set

A node-set is first converted into a string (as with string( )), then converted into a number by the rules for a string.

When called with no parameters, the converted value of the context node is returned.

The following example returns NaN:

```
number("three")
```

---

sum( )
returns the sum of all the nodes in the node-set operands

Parameters: node-set operands (required) **Defined in:** XPath 1.0
Return type: number

The value of each individual node is determined by converting the string-value to a number (as with number( )). If any individual node converts to NaN, the overall result is NaN.

For an XPath data model representing the following XML:

```
<operands>
  <operand>3.14</operand>
  <operand>42</operand>
  <operand>0</operand>
  <operand>0.86</operand>
</operands>
```

The following XPath expression returns 46:

```
sum(/operands/operand)
```

---

floor( )
returns the largest integer not greater than the num parameter

Parameters: number num (required) **Defined in:** XPath 1.0
Return type: number

(NaN, Infinity, and -Infinity are passed through unchanged.)

The first example returns 3, and the second example returns -4:

```
floor(3.14)
floor(-3.14)
```

---

ceiling( )
returns the smallest integer not less than the num parameter

Parameters: number num (required) **Defined in:** XPath 1.0
Return type: number

(NaN, Infinity, and -Infinity are passed through unchanged.)

The first example returns 4, and the second example returns -3:

```
ceiling(3.14)
ceiling(-3.14)
```

round( )

Parameters: number num (required)   **Defined in:** XPath 1.0
Return type: number

In the event of a tie, the larger result is returned. NaN, Infinity, and -Infinity are passed through unchanged.

The first example returns 4. The second example returns -3.

```
round(3.5)
round(-3.5)
```

boolean-from-string( )

Parameters: string bool (required)   **Defined in:** XForms 1.0
Return type: boolean

This function differs from boolean( ) in that it takes into account XML Schema rules: "true" or "1" produces true, and "false" or "0" produce false.

This example, as might be used when the value of the b element is of the type xs: boolean, returns an XPath boolean value that matches the XML Schema value of the node:

```
boolean-from-string(a/b)
```

if( )

Parameters: boolean test (required); string trueval   **Defined in:** XForms 1.0
(required); string falseval (required)
Return type: string

This function evaluates the boolean test parameter, and returns trueval if the test is true, or falseval otherwise. Note that all three parameters are always evaluated—no "short circuit" evaluation takes place.

If the evaluation of a/b yields true, this example returns "it worked", and otherwise returns "it failed":

```
if(boolean-from-string(a/b), "it worked", "it failed")
```

avg( )

returns the average of all the nodes in the node-set operands

Parameters: node-set operands (required)   **Defined in:** XForms 1.0
Return type: number

The average is computed as the sum( ) divided by the count( ) of the value of each individual node, converted into a number (as with number( )).

For an XPath data model representing the following XML:

```
<operands>
  <operand>3.14</operand>
  <operand>42</operand>
  <operand>0</operand>
  <operand>0.86</operand>
</operands>
```

The following XPath expression returns 11.5:

```
avg(/operands/operand)
```

min( )

returns the smallest of all the nodes in the node-set operands

Parameters: node-set operands (required)   **Defined in:** XForms 1.0
Return type: number

The value of each individual node is determined by converting the string-value to a number (as with number( )). A node-set that is empty or that includes nodes that evaluate to NaN will result in a return value of NaN.

For an XPath data model representing the following XML:

```
<operands>
  <operand>3.14</operand>
  <operand>42</operand>
  <operand>0</operand>
  <operand>0.86</operand>
</operands>
```

The following XPath expression returns 0:

```
min(/operands/operand)
```

max( )

returns the largest of all the nodes in the node-set operands

Parameters: node-set operands (required)   **Defined in:** XForms 1.0
Return type: number

The value of each individual node is determined by converting the string-value to a number (as with number( )). A node-set that is empty or that includes nodes that evaluate to NaN will result in a return value of NaN.

For an XPath data model representing the following XML:

```
<operands>
  <operand>3.14</operand>
```

```
<operand>42</operand>
<operand>0</operand>
<operand>0.86</operand>
</operands>
```

The following XPath expression returns 42:

```
max(/operands/operand)
```

---

count-non-empty( )   returns the count of all the non-empty nodes in the node-set operands

Parameters: node-set operands (required)   **Defined in:** XForms 1.0
Return type: number

For the purposes of this function, "non-empty" means a string-value of one or more characters. This can be useful when computing an average that disregards empty values.

For an XPath data model representing the following XML:

```
<operands>
<operand>3.14</operand>
<operand>42</operand>
<operand/>
<operand>0.86</operand>
</operands>
```

The following XPath expression returns 15.333333333333334:

```
sum(/operands/operand) div count-non-empty(/operands/operand)
```

---

index( )   returns the current index for a given repeat set

Parameters: string repeat-idref (required)   **Defined in:** XForms 1.0
Return type: number

XForms includes the notion of repeating content that holds a current index. This function is an accessor for that index.

A full example requires a "repeating structure" setup with XForms user interface markup. Further information and examples are available in Chapter 6.

---

property( )   returns the value of a given XForms property

Parameters: string propname (required)   **Defined in:** XForms 1.0
Return type: string

XForms specifies certain property strings that can be retrieved with this function:

- version returns the XForms version number
- conformance-level returns the XForms conformance level, either "basic" or "full"

This example returns 1.0, assuming the processing environment claims to be XForms 1.0 compliant:

```
property("version")
```

now( )

returns the current system date and time

Parameters: none   **Defined in:** XForms 1.0
Return type: string

The format returned by this function is a lexical XML Schema xs:dateTime format. If time zone information is unavailable from the system, an implementation default is used so that comparisons will still work.

This example returns 2003-02-14T09:13:02Z, when called at that point in time:

```
now( )
```

instance( )

provides access to an alternate XForms instance

Parameters: string instance-idref (required)   **Defined in:** XForms 1.0
Return type: node-set

XPath allows multiple separate instance data areas. This function returns the root node of the specified instance data. Normally, this function appears on the left-hand side of a path expression.

This example returns a node-set consisting of the rate element node from the instance named "taxtable":

```
instance('taxtable')/rate
```

days-from-date( )

converts an XML Schema xs:date into a signed whole number of days

Parameters: string date (required)   **Defined in:** XForms 1.0
Return type: number

This function computes a number of days relative to an epoch of 1970-01-01, and is most useful when two xs:date values need to be compared.

This example returns -1:

```
days-from-date("1969-12-31")
```

seconds-from-dateTime( )

converts an XML Schema xs:dateTime
into a number of seconds

Parameters: string dateTime (required)

Return type: number

Defined in: XForms 1.0

This function computes a signed fractional number of seconds relative to an epoch of 1970-01-01T00:00:00Z, and is useful when two xs:dateTimes need to be compared.

This example returns the large number of seconds representing the current date and time:

```
seconds-from-dateTime(now())
```

seconds( )

normalizes a dayTimeDuration into a number of seconds

Parameters: string dayTimeDuration (required)

Return type: number

Defined in: XForms 1.0

This function computes a fractional number of seconds that is equivalent in length to the dayTimeDuration parameter (formatted according to XML Schema rules).

This function makes the distinction of working on a dayTimeDuration, which is a more fine-grained datatype than defined by XML Schema. Chapter 4 discusses this in greater detail.

This example returns 297001.5:

```
seconds("P3DT10H30M1.5S")
```

months( )

normalizes a yearMonthDuration into a number of months

Parameters: string dayTimeDuration (required)

Return type: number

Defined in: XForms 1.0

This function computes a whole number of months that is equivalent in length to the yearMonthDuration parameter (formatted according to XML Schema rules).

This function makes the distinction of working on a yearMonthDuration, which is a more fine-grained datatype than defined by XML Schema. Chapter 4 discusses this in greater detail.

This example returns 14:

```
months("P1Y2M")
```

Extension Functions

The XPath specification itself is silent on the issue of implementation-specific or "extension" functions. XSLT, on the other hand, defines a framework in which extension functions can be used. Similarly, XForms provides a general outline of how extension functions fit in.

Extension functions are easily recognizable since all built-in functions are unprefixed names, while all extension functions contain a leading prefix and a colon character. A group of volunteers at the web site *http://www.exslt.org/* collect and maintain a number of extension functions that are suitable for use in XForms.

The main disadvantage of extension functions is non-portability. Since these functions are implementation-specific, any form that uses them will only work inside implementations that also support the functions used. To make this explicit, any form that uses extension functions should list the QNames of the functions in the `functions` attribute of the `model` element. For example, a form that needed a few more date and time functions from the EXSLT library would use the following declaration:

```
<xforms:model xmlns:exslt="http://exslt.org/dates-and-times"
functions="exslt:leap-year exslt:month-name exslt:day-name">
...
```

Upon initialization, the XForms Processor will check to make sure that all the listed functions are available and immediately signal an error if they are not. For this reason, only functions that are absolutely necessary to the proper functioning of the form should be listed here. On the other hand, failing to list a function here will likely cause a run-time XPath error in some implementations, such as when the user is filling out the form and gets to the point where the XPath engine will try (and fail) to locate the extension function.

How XPath is Used in XForms

Given a good understanding of what XPath is and how it works, it's pretty simple to see how it fits into the XForms architecture.

Context Nodes

Every use of XPath in XForms involves a context node, usually with the effect of shortening the number of steps needed in the path expression. For example, if the instance data is a simple XHTML document:

```
<html:html xmlns:html="http://www.w3.org/1999/html">
  <html:head>
```

```
    <html:title>Mutant Registration Guidelines</html:title>
  </html:head>
  <html:body>
    <html:p>The White House announced today...</html:p>
  </html:body>
</html:html>
```

the default context node is the element node named html:html. Thus, to bind a form control to the document title, instead of the longer absolute path /html:html/html:head/html:title, a shorter relative path html:head/html:title could be used. The key difference between the two is that absolute paths contain a leading slash and the name of the root element. Since there can be only one root element, including its name in every path expressions isn't necessary—path expressions don't become ambiguous by leaving out what is really a redundant step along the path.

The default context node can be changed. Any element containing a binding expressions resets the context node for any child elements. Binding expressions include the ref attribute possibly with the model attribute, or alternatively the bind attribute. Either way, the expression selects a node-set from the instance data, and the first node, in document order, is used as the context node for child elements. Chapter 10 shows a way to take advantage of this behavior to greatly simplify the use of XPath in XForms.

Within the markup for the XForms Model, there are a few things to be aware of regarding context nodes used for XPath expressions on the <bind> element. The nodeset attribute on this element selects an XPath node-set, applying certain properties such as calculate to each node. This means that the expression used will get evaluated multiple times, once for each node in the node-set. Upon each evaluation, the node being processed is the context node. This is most useful when a calculation appears in a repeating section. In the following example, each individual line item has a calculation that runs within the current line item only:

```
<!-- within each line item, calculate price times quantity -->
<xforms:bind nodeset="items/item/extension" calculate="../price * ../
quantity"/>
```

Another use for this processing is to automatically number nodes in document order, using the XPath function position( ), which returns the "context position," or the position of the node being processed relative to the entire node-set. For example, the following would sequentially number every line element in the instance data, placing the result in an attribute named line-number:

```
<!-- apply sequential numbering to line elements -->
<xforms:bind nodeset="lines/line/@line-number" calculate-"position( )"/>
```

In XPath, certain axes follow the reverse of document order: ancestor, ancestor-or-self, preceding, and preceding-sibling. Thus, an expression like preceding-sibling:: line[3] selects the 3rd line element node *backwards* from the context node.

Even when the nodeset attribute on bind contains such a reverse axis, however, the processing still happens in forward document order, including how nodes are counted with position( ). Due to the potential for confusion, it's probably best to completely avoid reverse axes in XForms.

Model Binding Expressions

A Model binding expression always appears on the attribute nodeset of the element bind. The expression must be a Location Path that returns a node-set. That node-set, in turn, is the target of all the model item properties, such as required or readonly, specified on the same bind element.

UI Binding Expressions

A UI binding expression always appears on a form control or user interface related component of XForms. Like a Model binding expression, it must be a Location Path that returns a node-set. There two possible attribute names, ref and nodeset, which are used to differentiate between processing that takes into account only the first node and the entire node-set, respectively.

Computations

In other places in XForms, an XPath expression is used as a lightweight scripting language. Such expressions are defined as taking various return datatypes. This usage of XPath is called a computed expression. Table 3-2 summarizes all computed expression used in XForms.

Table 3-2. Computed expression in XForms

Element	Attribute	Description	Datatype
bind	readonly	Determines whether a node is read-only	boolean
bind	required	Determines whether a node is required	boolean
bind	relevant	Determines whether a node is relevant	boolean
bind	constraint	Provides a predicate that must be satisfied for validity	boolean

Table 3-2. Computed expression in XForms (continued)

Element	Attribute	Description	Datatype
bind	calculate	Provides an automatically computed value for a node	string[a]
setvalue	value	Provides a one-time computed value for a node	string[b]
insert	at	Provides an index at which to insert new nodes	number
delete	at	Provides an index at which to delete nodes	number
output	value	Provides an automatically computed value for display	string

[a] A string as far as XPath is concerned, but must also match the XML Schema lexical datatype associated with that node to avoid causing form invalidation.
[b] As with calculate, the XPath string might have additional lexical constraints.

CHAPTER 4

XML Schema in XForms

*"Knowledge is of two kinds. We know a subject
ourselves, or we know where we can find
information on it."*
—Samuel Johnson

Forms and datatypes always seem to be mentioned together. It's natural to think of data entry in terms of specific types, such as date or phone number. Despite a feint in the opposite direction taken by earlier drafts, XForms incorporates the datatypes defined in W3C XML Schema. This chapter discusses these datatypes, and describes the general framework for describing and defining custom datatypes.

Wide Open (Value) Spaces

In describing a datatype, XML Schema distinguishes between a *lexical space*, or the data as it appears in XML, and a *value space*, or the data as it exists on an abstract level. In practice, many datatypes have a one-to-one mapping between the lexical space and the value space, so the distinction can seem a little academic. It is important, however, when there are equivalent representations for some value. For instance, the boolean datatype can represent true as either 1 or true, (and false as either 0 or false). Even though there are multiple possible representations, they both map to the underlying concept of *trueness* and *falseness*, respectively. This is important when comparing values; the value space is used as the basis for comparison.

Many observers have pointed out that the lexical representations of some XML Schema datatypes aren't very user friendly. As an example, the duration of a day and an hour is P1DT1H. From the perspective of the person filling out a form, this is complete gibberish. To work around this, XForms gives responsibility to individual form controls to present data to the user in a manner that's convenient to the intended audience. Thus, XForms introduces (but doesn't specifically name) a third space, the *user space*. For the benefit of users, this might not be a straightforward mapping—the form control can have great latitude in rearranging things, such as a graphical calendar control to enter durations and dates.

Derivation

XML Schema uses a divide-and-conquer technique to define datatypes. Each datatype can be broken down into a number of facets, each of which constrains some particular part of the allowed value space for that datatype. (One important exception is the pattern facet, which works on the lexical space.)

It's possible to take an existing datatype and trim it down to exactly meet your needs. This is called derivation by restriction, and entails changing one or more facets in the datatype. For example, the following XML Schema fragment limits the length of a string to 50 characters:

```
<xs:simpleType name="myString50">
  <xs:restriction base="xs:string">
    <xs:maxLength value="50"/>
  </xs:restriction>
</xs:simpleType>
```

This creates a new datatype named myString50, which can then be used in a form to limit the number of characters that can be entered. Other facets can similarly be restricted, as shown in the examples later in this chapter. The list of facets is as follows.

enumeration
Specifies a list of possible values.

fractionDigits
Specifies a number of digits after the decimal.

length
Specifies an exact length in characters, or bytes for binary datatypes.

maxExclusive
Specifies a maximum value that cannot be reached.

maxInclusive
Specifies a maximum value that can be reached.

maxLength
Specifies a maximum number of characters, or bytes for binary datatypes.

minExclusive
> Specifies a minimum value that can't be reached.

minExclusive
> Specifies a minimum value that can be reached.

minLength
> Specifies a minimum number of characters, or bytes for binary datatypes.

pattern
> Specifies a regular expression against the lexical space.

totalDigits
> Specifies the total number of significant digits.

whiteSpace
> Specifies how to handle whitespace.

Another kind of derivation is by list. This simply takes a simple datatype and produces a whitespace-separated list datatype. XForms includes a ready-made list datatype called listItems. Another variation is derivation by union, which can combine the value spaces of two separate datatypes. One final variation on derivation is by extension, which is used only in complexTypes, which are discussed later in this chapter.

Regular expressions

One of the most useful facet-based restrictions in forms is pattern, which takes a regular expression syntax, adjusted for Unicode compatibility. Entire books have been written on regular expression, so this section only covers the basics. For further information, a good source is Chapter 6 of Eric van der Vlist's *XML Schema* (O'Reilly).

When a regular expression contains letters or digits, the characters must appear in the entered data, as shown in Table 4-1.

Table 4-1. Simple regular expressions

Expression	Matches	Doesn't match
"hi"	"hi"	Any string other than "hi"

Oftentimes, you might know the format of a string but not the exact contents. For instance, a telephone number might be of the format 123-4567. To handle this, you can use escape sequences, which represent certain character types. Regular expressions support the escape sequences shown in Table 4-2.

Table 4-2. Escape sequences (case matters)

Sequence	Represents
. (dot)	Any Unicode character except newline
\w	Any word character
\W	Any non-word character
\d	Any digit character
\D	Any non-digit character
\s	Any whitespace character
\S	Any non-whitespace character
[abc]	Any character in the list abc
[a-z]	Any character between a and z in Unicode order
[^abc]	Any character not in the list abc
\p{UnicodeCharClass}	Any character that is part of UnicodeCharacterClass

The escape sequence \d matches more than just 0-9. It also matches many other characters considered numeric by Unicode, such as U+0A66 (Gurmukhi Digit Zero). While longer, specifying a pattern of [0-9] will give less surprise in some cases.

Regular expressions can also make use of the character classes shown in Table 4-3.

Table 4-3. Character classes

Expression	Matches	Doesn't match
\d	"3"	"X"
\w\w\w	"abc"	"ab1"
.\s.	"A 3"	"A3"
[abc]	"a"	"d"
[^a-f]	"X"	"f"
\pf{Lu} (Unicode upper case letters)	"A"	"a"

Using these, more complicated patterns are possible:

Since it quickly becomes tedious to repeat an escape sequence (e.g., representing a telephone number with \n\n\n-\n\n\n\n), regular expressions allow for partial matches, sequences, and repeat counts, as shown in Table 4-4.

Table 4-4. Quantifiers

Quantifier	Represents
? (dot)	Repeat zero or once (optional)
+	Repeat one or more
*	Repeat zero or more
{*n*}	Repeat exactly *n* times
{*n,m*}	Repeat between *n* and *m* times
{*n,*}	Repeat *n* or more times

Using quantifiers, more complicated types of expressions are possible. Also, parentheses can be used for grouping, and the vertical bar (|) to express two possible branches, either one of which can satisfy the expression, as shown in Table 4-5.

Table 4-5. Regular expressions with quantifiers

Expression	Matches	Doesn't match
\w\d?\w	"b1b"	"bbb"
\w\d*	"a123"	"1234"
\w\s+\w	"c c"	"cc"
\d{4,5}	"31415"	"314159"
[bcd]{3,}	"bbbb"	"ab"
0x[0-9A-F]{4}	"0xBEEF"	"0x0A"
[0-9]{5}(-[0-9]{4})?	"90210" or "90210-1241"	"90210-"
\d{3}|[a-z]{4}	"123" or "dbca"	"1234" or "cba"

The final thing to remember is that characters otherwise used for something else need to be escaped when used literally. These characters, in their escaped form, are \\; \|; \.; \-; \^; \?; *; \+; \{; \}; \(; \); \[; and \].

Table 4-6 provides a few ready-to-use regular expressions, suitable for copy-and-paste.

Table 4-6. Regular expressions: complete examples

Expression	Description
\+\d{2}\s\d{4}\s\d{6}	Matches an international phone number, such as "+12 1234 123456"
\d{3}-\d{4}	Matches a 7-digit phone number, such as "123-4567"
\d{3}-\d{4}(x\d{2,6})?	Matches a 7-digit phone number, with an optional 2-6 digit extension
\d{3}-\d{2}-\d{4}	Matches a US Social Security number

Table 4-6. Regular expressions: complete examples (continued)

Expression	Description
\w+@\w+\.\w+	Simplistic email address check
X\d{4}	Matches part numbers formatted like "X1234"
\p{Lu}+(\s+\p{Lu}+)*	Matches one or more space-separated uppercase words

Useful Datatypes

The following useful datatypes are either part of the XForms specification, or included from XML Schema. For each datatype, this section describes where it is defined, what conformance level of XForms it applies to, how the datatype is useful, caveats, and one or more examples.

xs:string   Defined in: XML Schema part 2

As the least-restricted datatype, xs:string is the default datatype that XForms will use, unless the author specifies otherwise.

Caveats

xs:string punts on all whitespace processing, so all tab characters and newline characters pass through unchanged. If this is undesired, it is better to use a more restricted datatype such as xs:normalizedString or xforms:listItem.

Example

• Hello, World

xs:normalizedString   Defined in: XML Schema part 2

The only difference between this datatype and xs:string is that all whitespace characters are converted into space (0x20) characters.

Caveats

Whitespace is normalized, but not collapsed. Thus, it is still possible for multiple consecutive whitespace characters to exist.

Example

• Hello, World

xs:language

If a form collects the name of a human language, this is the datatype to use.

Caveats

The actual values that represent languages are subject to change over time.

Examples

- en
- en-US
- x-sindarin

xs:boolean

Simple on/off controls, such as a single checkbox, are naturally represented by a boolean datatype.

Caveats

The lexical space allows multiple representations, so any script or XPath function that reads a value of this datatype should be prepared to see either a string ("true" or "false") or a number (1 or 0).

Examples

- true
- 1
- false
- 0

xs:decimal

Any decimal number can be exactly represented by this datatype.

Caveats

The definition of this datatype defines no restrictions whatsoever on the size of numbers permissible under this datatype. Unless your form processing is prepared to deal with a number thousands of digits long (or even longer), you should use a restriction on the allowed upper and lower limits, and number of digits past the decimal point, as shown here:

```
<xs:simpleType name="restrictedInteger">
  <xs:restriction base="xs:decimal">
    <xs:maxExclusive value="1000000"/>
    <xs:minInclusive value="-1000000"/>
```

```
        <xs:fractionDigits value='2'/>
    </xs:restriction>
</xs:simpleType>
```

Examples

- 3.14
- -123456789012345678901234567890123456789012345
- 0.318309886

---

xs:integer   Defined in: XML Schema part 2

This datatype is derived from xs:decimal, with the restriction that only whole numbers are permitted.

Caveats

As with xs:decimal, there is no inherent upper bound on the size of this datatype.

Examples

- 0
- 123456
- -42

---

xs:nonPositiveInteger   Defined in: XML Schema part 2

This datatype is derived from xs:integer, with the restriction that positive values are not allowed.

Caveats

The same warnings about length of the lexical representation from xs:integer apply here.

Examples

- 0
- -1234

---

xs:negativeInteger   Defined in: XML Schema part 2

This datatype is derived from xs:integer, with the restriction that only negative values are allowed.

Caveats

The same warnings about length of the lexical representation from xs:integer apply here.

Examples

- -1
- -9078563412

---

xs:nonNegativeInteger   Defined in: XML Schema part 2

This datatype is derived from xs:integer, with the restriction that negative values are not allowed.

Caveats

The same warnings about length of the lexical representation from xs:integer apply here.

Examples

- 0
- 9078563412

---

xs:positiveInteger   Defined in: XML Schema part 2

This datatype is derived from xs:integer, with the restriction that only positive values are allowed.

Caveats

The same warnings about length of the lexical representation from xs:integer apply here.

Examples

- 42
- 9078563412

---

xs:double   Defined in: XML Schema part 2

This datatype maps directly to the XPath concept of number, and thus can be useful in situations where data flows back and forth between XPath and the XML instance data.

Caveats

Unlike the decimal datatypes, xs:double is based on an internal binary representation, so many operations (particularly comparisons) are only approximations. The lexical space of this datatype allows scientific notation, so you need to be careful not to assume that any particular representation will always be used. Also, special values of NaN (not a number), INF (infinity), -INF (negative infinity), as well as negative zero, are possible. NaN in particular behaves strangely in comparisons, being equal to itself and greater than all other numbers, even INF!

Examples

- 3.14159
- 3.14159E0
- NaN
- 0
- -0
- INF
- -INF

---

xs:dateTime
Defined in: XML Schema part 2

This datatype identifies a specific moment in time.

Caveats

Having our planet divided into time zones complicates matters, since one xs:dateTime with a time zone can't always be reliably compared to another without time zone information.

Example

- 2002-07-30T23:32:15.32-09:00

---

xs:time
Defined in: XML Schema part 2

This datatype identifies a recurring point in time each day.

Caveats

The same time zone warnings apply as with other date and time datatypes. Additionally, keep in mind that this format is not useful for representing a duration.

Example

- 21:37:32-08:00

---

xs:date

Defined in: XML Schema part 2

This datatype identifies a particular period of time one day long.

Caveats

An optional time zone identifier on the end complicates matters, as is the case with xs:dateTime.

Example

- 2002-07-30-09:00

xs:base64Binary

Defined in: XML Schema part 2

This datatype allows characters, including control characters, that otherwise aren't representable in XML.

Caveats

Base64 encoding increases the size of any encoded data.

Example

- Q2VjaSBuJ2VzdCBwYXMgdW4gZW5jb2Rpbmc=

xs:anyURI

Defined in: XML Schema part 2

This datatype represents a URI, which includes web page addresses (commonly called URLs).

Caveats

The allowed characters in anyURI include spaces and other characters not usually found in URI syntax.

Examples

- http://dubinko.info/writing/xforms/
- file://localhost/My Documents/résumé
- mailto:editors@xmlhack.com

xforms:yearMonthDuration

Defined in: XForms 1.0

This datatype represents a duration of a certain number of months (and therefore years also).

Caveats

It's not possible to combine smaller durations, such as days, with xforms:
yearMonthDuration without introducing ambiguity. For instance, a month and a
day could be anywhere between 29 and 32 days.

Examples

- P1Y2M
- P21M

---

xforms:dayTimeDuration
Defined in: XForms 1.0

This datatype represents a duration of a certain number of seconds (and from
that, a number of days, hours, and minutes can be determined).

Caveats

It's not possible to combine larger durations, such as years, with xforms:
dayTimeDuration without introducing ambiguity.

Examples

- PT10000001S
- P4DT3H2M1S

---

xforms:listItem
Defined in: XForms 1.0

This datatype represents only non-whitespace characters, and thus makes an
excellent base type for a whitespace-separated list datatype (namely xforms:
listItems).

Caveats

None

Examples

- vanilla
- noauto,owner,kudzu

---

xforms:listItems
Defined in: XForms 1.0

This datatype represents a space-separated list, and can be used directly with
XForms list form controls.

Caveats

None.

Examples

- Hello World
- 0 1 0 1 1 1 null

Other Datatypes

The datatypes in the following list are less useful in forms, except perhaps in unusual circumstances. Nevertheless, they are a part of XForms, and are included here for completeness. Besides, someone might discover new ways to use these datatypes.

xs:float Defined in: XML Schema part 2

The datatype xs:double can do anything xs:float can do and more. If you need to capture floating point values, use xs:double.

xs:duration Defined in: XML Schema part 2

As specified, many duration comparisons are indeterminate. For example, is a month equal to 30 days? The answer varies from month to month. Because of this, XForms suggests against using xs:duration, except as an abstract base type for xforms:dayTimeDuration and xforms:yearMonthDuration. These derived types should always be used instead of xs:duration.

"gHorribleKluge"
xs:gYearMonth, xs:gYear, xs:gMonthDay, xs:gDay, xs:gMonth   Defined in: XML Schema part 2

These datatypes, thanks to their generally awkward natures, have collectively been christened "gHorribleKluge" by folks on the xml-dev mailing list. Very few XML documents are defined using these datatypes, which use a truncated representation of the ISO 8601 representation embodied in xs:date.

xs:hexBinary Defined in: XML Schema part 2

This type is intended to contain bytes represented as hexadecimal values. However, in cases that absolutely require binary data to be encoded inline in XML, it is better to use the more compact xs:base64Binary.

Computer-centric numbers

xs:long, xs:unsignedLong, xs:int, xs:unsignedInt, xs:short,
xs:unsignedShort, xs:byte, xs:unsignedByte　　　　　Defined in: XML Schema part 2

From the perspective of someone filling out a form, the boundary conditions
inherent in a computer's internal number system are irrelevant, as is the distinction between "signed" and "unsigned" numbers. Unless you are creating a form
that deals with numbers that are naturally bounded by 8, 16, 32, or 64-bit representations, use `xs:integer` or `xs:decimal`.

Markup datatypes

xs:NOTATION, xs:token, xs:Name, xs:NCName, xs:NMTOKEN,
xs:ID, xs:IDREF, xs:ENTITY, xs:ENTITIES, xs:QName　　　Defined in: XML Schema part 2

From the perspective of someone filling out a form, details of XML internals such
as NMTOKENs or IDREFs shouldn't matter. Even `xs:token` (which should have
been named `xs:tokenized`) allows whitespace within the value and doesn't map to
anything typical users would enter in a form. Unless you are creating a form that
deals directly with XML data structures, choose different datatypes.

Further, `xs:NOTATION`, `xs:ENTITY`, and `xs:ENTITIES` are not guaranteed to be
supported at all in XForms, and thus should be studiously avoided.

An Email Datatype for XForms

One of the great disappointments in the XForms specification is the lack of a
defined datatype for email—the one datatype common to nearly every Web
form. Even if the specification doesn't define an email datatype, form
designers still can. Getting all the details right is a little tricky, though. Since
regular expressions aren't a programming language, there's no way to define
a common recurring segment, and the regular expression tends to get a little
repetitive. Taken one step at a time, however, it makes perfect sense. The
datatype definition conforming to RFC 2822 is:

```
<xs:simpleType name="email">
  <xs:restriction base="xs:string">
    <xs:pattern value="[A-Za-z0-9!#-'\*\+\-/=\?\^_`\{-~]+
        (\.[A-Za-z0-9!#-'\*\+\-/=\?\^_`\{-~]+)*@[A-Za-z0-9!#-
        '\*\+\-/=\?\^_`\{-~]+(\.[A-Za-z0-9!#-'\*\+\-/=\?\^_`\
        {-~]+)*"/>
  </xs:restriction>
</xs:simpleType>
```

The main achievement in this lengthy statement is the definition of what the email address specification calls *atext*, which is defined alpha characters, digits, or one of the following characters:

"!" "#" "$" "%" "&" "'" "*" "+" "-" "/" "=" "?" "^" "_" "`" "{" "|" "}" "~"

In regular expression syntax, the definition for a single character of atext looks like this:

```
[A-Za-z0-9!#-'\*\+\-/=\?\^_`\{-~]
```

Note that the character ranges in this expression prevent it from being even bulkier, and that a number of the characters used need to be escaped. If you compare this with the entire regular expression given earlier, you will see that this definition repeats four times overall. If regular expressions had a way to define a commonly-recurring string, the regular expression might look like this (with spaces added for readability):

```
atext+ (\. atext+)* @ atext+ (\. atext+)*
```

But alas, the actual regular expression needs to repeat the full definition of atext four times, yielding the full definition of the email datatype.

Using the Email Datatype

This datatype definition is available online, so any XForms definition that includes the XML Schema at *http://dubinko.info/writing/xforms/email.xsd* will be able to support email datatypes in forms.

```
<xforms:model schema="http://dubinko.info/writing/xforms/datatypes.xsd">
...
```

Complex Types

In XML Schema, a *complex type* is a datatype definition that can include element structure and attributes, which makes possible a number of additional (and, yes, complex) features including substitution groups, redefinition, and complex derivation. XForms includes the whole of XML Schema, though an easier-to-process profile that will leave out the complicated parts is still under development.

In many cases, the XML that will be processed by XForms already has a pre-existing XML Schema. In such cases it makes good sense to re-use the Schema by referencing it from the XForms Model. By doing so, additional datatype information will be made available to XForms.

If a Schema doesn't already exist, however, it's generally better to define only the minimum needed datatypes and leave it at that. The main reason for this recommendation is that many devices—those that adhere to a simpler XForms profile—will ignore all these more complicated features, and that any form that relies on them will produce different answers, depending on whether an XForms Full or XForms Basic device is accessing them.

For example, a Schema might define a coarse complexType that gets redefined into one with stricter validations. These stricter validations won't be seen by XForms Basic, and thus the unsuspecting person filling out the form might enter wrong values and have no idea they're even making a mistake.

xsi:type

One contested feature of XML Schema is an attribute named xsi:type, which can be placed directly on XML instance data elements, even if a preexisting Schema doesn't permit the attribute.* For existing XML that uses this with simpleTypes, such as those described earlier in this chapter, this is a reasonable course. If the xsi:type identifies a complexType, however, all the problems in the previous section apply. For new development, the less intrusive XForms type model item property should be used, as described at Chapter 5.

---

* In fact, it's not even possible in XML Schema to define where xsi:type attributes should or should not be allowed.

CHAPTER 5

The XForms Model

ARTHUR: Camelot!
GALAHAD: Camelot!
LANCELOT: Camelot!
PATSY: It's only a model.
ARTHUR: Shhh!
—Monty Python and the Holy Grail

The term *data model* is probably one of the most terrifying and confusing terms[*] to ever get written in a Web specification. That's why the XForms specification goes to great lengths to avoid that term. Instead, *XForms Model* is the name given to the form description. That name was chosen mainly because it wasn't "data model," but also to evoke thoughts of the Model-View-Controller (MVC) design pattern in programming. In MVC, a model contains all the essential data, and one or more views provide a viewpoint to examine or interact with the data. The XForms Model is analogous to a MVC model, and form controls, covered in Chapter 6, serve the function of views. (There's nothing that directly maps to a controller in XForms, though portions of the processing model and XForms Events play a similar role.)

Will the Real Data Model Step Forward?

XForms is based on a foundation data model, but you won't find it defined anywhere in the XForms specification. Instead, the XForms data model subsumes the XPath data model, which maps nodes to various structures in

---

[*] It doesn't help the situation any when the term *infoset* is often used interchangably with data model.

XML: elements, attributes, text, comments, processing instructions, namespaces, and a special node representing the document root. Chapter 3 describes this data model in great detail. This data model, resulting from parsed XML, is the source of nodes used in XForms.

A later section of this chapter describes the instance element, which can either point to or directly contain XML. Either way, this XML is parsed to create nodes in the instance data. (Another possibility is during "lazy author" processing, where the instance data nodes are built from scratch, without need of any author-provided XML.) The distinction between instance and instance data is subtle; a good comparison might be between the hard markup in a web page, as seen with the View Source command, and the in-memory representation accessible from the DOM. In nearly every case, XForms works from the internal instance data, ignoring the document markup. As a consequence, selecting View Source in the browser will always show the document as it was when it initially loaded, and any changes made because of XForms activity won't be visible.

A solid foundation is important, but useless without anything built on top of it. A major reason for XForms having been created in the first place is to provide useful features, such as automatic recalculation or validation. To accomplish these things in XForms, two pieces are needed in addition to the XPath foundation:

- A set of properties for calculation, validation, etc.
- A way to connect the properties to user form controls.

A *model item* is the name for an XPath node with the addition of certain XForms properties, formally called *model item properties*. The connection between model item properties and form controls is called *binding*, which is accomplished through a set of XML elements that comprise the XForms Model. The next section describes these elements.

Structural Elements

The XForms Model is made up of a number of different elements, outlined here.

The model Element

This element is the local root of the definition of the XForms Model. It is typically found in a non-rendered area of the containing document.

In the following example, the head section in XHTML can contain an XForms Model.

```
<html xmlns="http://www.w3.org/1999/xhtml" xmlns:xforms="http://www.w3.org/
2002/xforms">
  <head>
    <title>A sample XHTML+XForms document</title>
    <xforms:model>
      ...more XForms elements...
    </xforms:model>
  </head>
  <body>
    ...
```

The attribute functions declares any extension functions, as covered in Chapter 11, that are absolutely necessary for the form to function.

The attribute schema includes a space-separated list of external XML Schema documents to be retrieved and included in the definition of the XForms Model. Additionally, XML Schema definitions may occur inline, with one or more xs: schema elements appearing as children of the model element. As Chapter 6 will describe, the datatype associated with a node can have an effect on the user interface presented to the user for populating the node with data.

Since the model element is a target of several kinds of events (see Chapter 7), XML Events attributes are also permitted in this element.

The instance Element

This element serves as a container for initial instance data.

The instance element has a unique restriction on the single allowed child element: absolutely anything, in any namespace, is allowed, as long as it would make a well-formed XML document if it existed in a separate file. The content is treated as "opaque," which means that even if the child element (or any descendants) contain elements that would normally affect the operation of the document (including nested XForms elements), the elements don't invoke any special processing. The contents of this element are simply data that will be both read and written during form interaction, nothing more.

Instead of inline content, instance may use Linking Attributes (that is to say, src) to point to external instance data. Other than requiring an extra network fetch operation, behavior in this case is exactly the same.

The bind Element

This element establishes conditions that are continuously applied to the instance data.

With instance data defined neatly by the instance element, the question remains of how to annotate instance data nodes with properties necessary for forms. Chapter 5 describes these model item properties but, for now, it is sufficient to know that each model item property is represented by an attribute on this element.

- type
- readonly
- required
- relevant
- calculate
- constraint
- p3ptype

The properties are applied through an additional attribute, nodeset, which, not surprisingly, selects a node-set. For each node in the selected node-set, model item properties are initialized according to the corresponding attribute value. If two separate bind elements are configured to set conflicting model item properties on the same node, an error condition will result, preventing the form from operating.

The submission Element

This will be covered in Chapter 8.

Common Attributes

The techniques in *Modularization of XHTML* provide a mechanism to assemble and name common groups of attributes that can be easily referenced. The following sections describe these attribute groups.

Binding Attributes—Single Node and Node-set

A number of situations in XForms call for a reference into instance data. The term for such attributes is *binding attributes*, which include up to three attributes from this list:

ref
> Whenever the intent of the binding attributes is to select a single node, the ref attribute will be present. It contains an XPath path expression. In cases where the selected node-set happens to have more than one node, the *first node rule* applies, which removes all nodes other than the first, according to the order the nodes appear in the document.

nodeset
> Whenever the intent of the binding attributes is to select a node-set of any size, the nodeset attribute will be present. It contains an XPath path expression.

model

In larger or more complex documents, it will be common to have multiple XForms Models. When this is the case, an additional attribute is needed to indicate to which XForms Model the binding attaches. The value of this attribute is of type IDREF, and so a model element in the same document must have an attribute of type ID with a matching value.

bind

In some cases, such as when a graphic design professional who isn't concerned with XPath is laying out a form, it isn't desirable to have XPath strewn about on every set of binding attributes. The bind attribute, which takes precedence over any of ref, nodeset, or model, refers back to an already-defined node-set on a bind element. The value of this attribute is of type IDREF, and so a bind element in the same document must have an attribute of type ID with a matching value.

It's worth noting that the term binding, as used in XForms, can refer to two separate things. *UI Binding* occurs on an attribute of a form control element, and binds the form control to a particular model item. In dynamic forms, the association to a model item can jump around, causing the form control to be a window to different parts of the data at different times. The other use of binding, *Model Binding,* occurs on the element bind, selecting an entire node-set to which a set of model item properties gets applied. It is a serious problem to have a dynamic model binding expression, since that complicates life behind-the-scenes for an XForms Processor, which can cause difficult-to-detect errors.

Model Item Properties

An individual property that can be applied to a node is called a *model item property.* Some of the properties are XPath expressions (called *computed expressions* in the specification), which the XForms Processor tracks and reevaluates as necessary:

- readonly
- required
- relevant
- calculate
- constraint

The remaining properties are static, and don't get reevaluated:

- type
- p3ptype

Some of the model item properties have an effect on child nodes as well. The rules for this behavior can be summarized like this:

- Setting a node to readonly sets all child nodes to readonly, unless specifically overridden.
- Setting a node to non-relevant sets all child nodes to non-relevant, unless specifically overridden.
- For all other model item properties, setting that property on a node has no effect on child nodes.

A common mistake is to write code like this:

```
required="true"
```

This almost certainly doesn't have the intended effect of making the node always required. Computed model item properties are XPath expressions, and under XPath rules, "true" is interpreted as a node-set matching all element nodes named true. Unless there is such an element, the expression will evaluate to an empty node-set, which is interpreted as an XPath boolean false! Always use the functions true( ) and false( ), which return the expected XPath boolean values.

```
required="true( )"
```

type

Allowed values: a xs:QName representing an available XML Schema datatype.
Default value: xs:string

This property associates an XML Schema datatype with an instance data node.

The unusual thing about this property is that it's technically unnecessary. The right XML Schema incantations can accomplish the same result. In many cases, however, using this model item property is more convenient than using XML Schema features.

Attaching a datatype to an element node is the most straightforward scenario. XML Schema provides an instance-based syntax, using an xsi:type attribute that can be attached to any element. The main drawbacks of this technique are that it is highly intrusive to the instance data and that it works only with elements.

Normal XML Schema conventions can also be used to associate a datatype with a node, and this works with attributes, too. For example, the following XML Schema fragment associates a datatype of my:phoneNum to an attribute named pn:

```
<xs:attribute name="pn" type="my:phoneNum"/>
```

readonly

Allowed values: any XPath expression; the result is interpreted as a boolean.
Default value: false

This property signals whether a node is read-only, in which case form controls attached to the node won't allow the user to change data.

Form controls take a hint from the readonly property and are expected to distinctly render a read-only condition; for example, by dimming the form control.

required

Allowed values: any XPath expression; the result is interpreted as a boolean.
Default value: false

This property signals whether a value is required in this node for the form to be considered valid. A node satisfies the required condition when it is convertible into a string with one or more characters.

Form controls take a hint from the required property. Form controls are required to distinguish between valid and invalid states, and satisfying this property is a part of validity.

relevant

Allowed values: any XPath expression; the result is interpreted as a boolean.
Default value: true

This property signals whether a node is currently relevant to the form. Form controls bound to non-relevant nodes are either disabled or completely invisible. Non-relevant nodes are not even submitted with the rest of the data.

Form controls are directly affected by this property, and will be disabled or hidden depending on the implementation. One interaction to watch out for is when a non-relevant field is required. In that case, the required property won't hold, although if the node were to become relevant again, it would still be required.

calculate

Allowed values: any XPath expression; the result is interpreted as a string.
Default value: none

This property defines a calculation used to determine the value of the node.

It's important that interrelated calculations run in the proper order, and XForms takes care of this by analyzing the dependencies and correctly ordering the individual computations.

It's not wise to attach an editable form control to a calculated node, since the XForms specification gives recalculation engines the freedom to recalculate at nearly any given time. As part of the recalculation processing, any new information entered into the form control will get wiped out.

constraint

Allowed values: any XPath expression; the result is interpreted as a boolean.
Default value: `true`

This property imposes an additional XPath-based constraint on the validity of the attached node.

If the XPath expression with this property evaluates to `false`, the attached node is guaranteed to be invalid. If it evaluates to `true`, however, it's still possible (through XML Schema constraints) that the attached node might be invalid.

---

minOccurs and maxOccurs

Earlier drafts of the XForms Specification included model item properties for `minOccurs` and `maxOccurs`, designed to restrict the number of times a repeated node could occur. Difficulties arose in describing how these would actually work, since any given sequence of repeating nodes could have differing restrictions on each node.

Such restrictions can still be done with the `calculate` property, as shown in this example, which restricts the number of item children to more than zero and less than ten:

```
<xforms:bind nodeset="items" constraint="count(item) &gt; 0 and
count(item) &lt; 10"/>
```

---

p3ptype

Allowed values: any valid P3P datatype identifier.
Default value: `none`

This property associates a P3P datatype identifier with a node.

The Platform for Privacy Preferences (P3P) is a W3C specification that describes a machine-readable profile of what personally identifiable information is collected by a web site—especially forms. The main use of this property is to give P3P-compliant browsers enough information, at a granular enough level, to offer users flexible choices in how much personal information they give out, and to whom. Another use of this property is as a key for autocomplete features. IE6 and Netscape 6 already both have the capability to remember things entered into forms, but matching the right data to the right part of the form has always been hit-or-miss. With the rich expressive capability of P3P datatypes, this problem is a thing of the past.

Making the Connection—Binding

The remaining detail is how to associate model item properties with particular instance data nodes. The answer is binding, but it's worth being extra clear with terminology: a bind has two ends, one side in the XForms Model, and the other side at a form control. On the bind element within the XForms Model, the nodeset attribute holds the Model Binding Expression. On the other end, in the user interface, is the UI Binding Expression. This end may be bound two ways, using either IDREFs or XPath.

With IDREFs

The recommended way to perform binding is to put an id attribute on each bind element, and refer back to this with a bind attribute on each form control:

```
<!-- in the XForms Model -->
<xforms:bind nodeset="email" id="mybind" required="true()"/>
...
<!-- later in the document -->
<xforms:input bind="mybind"...>
```

This approach is distinguished by the use of the bind attribute on form controls. The main advantage of this approach is that it maintains separation between the model and the view. If the structure of the instance data were to change, only the attributes on the bind elements would need to be updated. In large organizations, form authoring often involves separate teams: a graphic design team to lay out the form, and a systems team to handle the data integration. In such scenarios, IDREF binding provides a perfect interface between content and presentation.

With XPath

Another way to bind is with XPath expressions on the form controls:

```
<!-- in the XForms Model -->
<xforms:bind nodeset="email" id="mybind" required="true( )"/>
...
<!-- later in the document -->
<xforms:input ref="email"...>
```

This approach is distinguished by the use of ref attributes on form controls. Many view this approach as simpler, since it cuts out one level of indirection. It is also more fragile, however, since the XPath expressions to locate nodes appear in two places. If the structure of the instance data were to change, both the attributes on the bind element and the ref attributes on the form controls would need to change.

Multiple Models

It's common to have multiple forms in the same document, and thus have multiple XForms Models. The document markup for this is straightforward:

```
<!-- in the XForms Model 1 -->
<xform:model id="m1">
  <xforms:bind nodeset="email" type="my:email"/>
  ...
</xforms:model>

<xforms:model id="m2">
  <xforms:bind nodeset="search" type="my:query"/>
  ...
</xforms:model>

<!-- later in the document -->
<xforms:input ref="email" model="m1"...>
<xforms:input ref="search" model="m2"...>
```

When using IDREF binding, this causes no additional problems, since the ID the form control points to is necessarily unique in the document. When using XPath binding, however, additional information is needed. In which model do you find purchaseOrder/items/item[2]? Because of this dilemma, in any document with two or more XForms Models, every XPath-style binding needs an additional attribute, model, to indicate which model is being bound to. By design, each XForms Model is a self-contained unit, and options for cross-model communication are limited.

Multiple Instances

A common scenario is that a form needs some extra data, perhaps for a calculation. In HTML forms, hidden fields could be used for this. But in XForms, the initial form data is XML, which is already widely deployed. Often, it's not possible to modify existing DTDs and XML Schemas to add new forms-specific elements and attributes to legacy XML. In these cases, it is possible to set aside additional XForms Instances as temporary storage.

On the markup side, this, too, is straightforward—using multiple instance elements:

```
<!-- in the XForms Model -->
<xforms:model>
  <xforms:instance id="formdata">
    <my:root>
      ...
    </my:root>
  </xforms:instance>
  <xforms:instance id="userid" src="scripts/getuserid"/>
  ...
  <xforms:bind nodeset="my:root/..."/>
  <xforms:bind nodeset="instance('userid')/..."/>
  ...
</xforms:model>
```

A similar problem to having multiple models occurs when you try to write a XPath expression that reaches across instances. By default, XPath expressions will always point into the first instance. The function instance( ), which takes an IDREF of an instance element, resets the XPath context to a different instance (but always within the same XForms Model).

The XForms User Interface

*"A human being should be able to change a diaper, plan
an invasion, butcher a hog, conn a ship, design a
building, write a sonnet, balance accounts, build a wall,
set a bone, comfort the dying, take orders, give orders,
cooperate, act alone, solve equations, analyze a new
problem, pitch manure, program a computer, cook a
tasty meal, fight efficiently, and die gallantly.
Specialization is for insects."*
—Robert A. Heinlein

Form controls are windows onto the form data kept in the XForms Model.
In principle, this was true also for HTML forms, although the design of
XForms makes a much sharper separation.

Form Controls

The following sections describe every form control included in XForms. The
examples show a variety of different binding techniques through the
attributes ref, model, and bind, which are explained in Chapter 5.

input

This form control is quite similar to its HTML forms counterpart, as it permits the entry of any character data. There are some significant improvements, however, such as the ability to use an XML Schema datatype to
optimize the user experience of entering the data. Example 6-1 shows sample code for an entry control, and Figure 6-1 shows several different render-

ings, selected by datatype, of an input control in the open source X-Smiles browser, available at *http://www.x-smiles.org*.

Example 6-1. Sample markup for an input control

```
<input ref="string"> <!-- bound to node with XML Schema type xs:string -->
  <label>xsd:string</label>
</input>
<input ref="date"> <!-- bound to node with XML Schema type xs:date -->
  <label>Ship By:</label>
</input>
```

Figure 6-1. Input form controls rendered with X-Smiles

- The presentation isn't limited to a standard edit box. The XForms specification includes an example where a date control can be entered through a calendar interface.

- Even when using standard character entry, the form control will adjust the presentation to meet the user's expectations. For example, even though a decimal number is always specified as 1234.56 in XML, it might be presented to the user as 1.234,56 or 1,234.56, depending on locale settings in the browser or operating system.

- As is the case with all form controls, input keeps track of the notion of validity, and continuously informs the user of the validity status of the data in the controls.

Almost any simpleType can bind to input, except the binary datatypes, like base64Binary, which don't make sense for manual entry and aren't allowed.

secret

This form control is nearly identical to its HTML forms counterpart. It offers only a cursory level of security, since the collected data isn't encrypted in any way, merely obscured for presentation. For end-to-end security, additional measures such as SSL are necessary. Example 6-2 shows sample markup for a secret control, and Figure 6-2 shows the result in the Orbeon OXF processor, available at *http://www.orbeon.com/oxf/doc/processors-xforms*.

Example 6-2. Sample markup for a secret control

```
<secret ref="/session/password">
  <label>Password</label>
</secret>
```

Figure 6-2. Secret form control rendered with OXF

Data binding for this control follows the same rules as input.

textarea

This form control is also very close to its HTML forms counterpart. The main difference between this form control and input is that textarea is optimized for larger, usually multiple line, stretches of text. Example 6-3 shows sample markup for a textarea control, and Figure 6-3 shows the rendering using the IBM XML Forms Package, available at *http://www.alphaworks.ibm.com/tech/xmlforms*.

Example 6-3. Sample markup for a textarea control

```
<textarea ref="/msg:Message/mime:Body">
  <label>Message Body:</label>
</textarea>
```

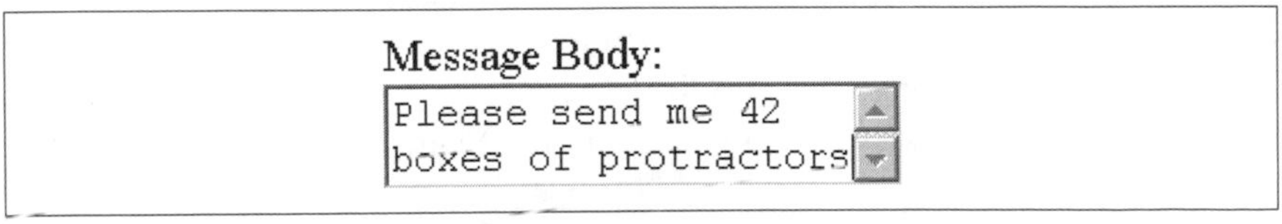

> **Message Body:**
> ```
> Please send me 42
> boxes of protractors
> ```

Figure 6-3. Textarea form control rendered with the IBM XML Forms Package

Data binding for this control follows the same rules as input.

output

This is the only form control that doesn't accept user input, though once developers start using it, they can't imagine life without it. output renders data from an XForms Model as inline text, normally indistinguishable from other text on the page. The same transformations that apply to text rendered in an input form control apply equally to output so that, for instance, numeric values will be correctly formatted to user expectations. Example 6-4 shows sample markup for an output control. Since the result of an output control is ordinary inline text, screen shots tend to be rather unimpressive.

Example 6-4. Sample markup for an output control

```
<output ref="/my:employee/my:name">
  <label>Name:</label>
</output>
<input ref="/my:employee/my:name">
  <label>Edit the name here:</label>
</input>
```

Figure 6-4 shows an output control alongside an input control, to demonstrate how it operates, running in the Mozquito DENG "Desktop Engine," available at *http://mozquito.markuplanguage.net*.

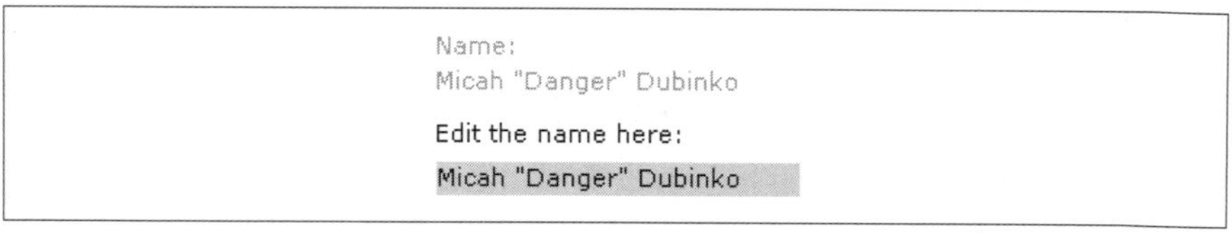

Figure 6-4. Output form control rendered with DENG

A couple of other design aspects of output stand out. For one, a label element is not required, for situations where only the dynamic content is required. The actual content taken from the instance data is rendered, usually in an inline manner that isn't stylistically distinguishable from surrounding text.

In some cases, the value to be displayed doesn't relate directly to an instance data node, but rather needs to be computed. To handle this common case, the attribute value, containing any XPath expression, can be used instead of the ref attribute, which can contain only an XPath path selection expression.

This control can bind to any simpleType, although it's not clear how binary items would be supported. Presumably, binary items, such as images, could be rendered as the content of this element.

upload

HTML forms had a limited file upload control, but the XForms version surpasses it in many ways. Example 6-5 shows sample code for an upload control, and Figure 6-5 shows the result rendered in X-Port's FormsPlayer, available at *http://www.formsplayer.com*.

Example 6-5. Sample markup for the upload control

```
<upload bind="attachment1">
  <label>Select a file</label>
  <filename bind="fname1"/>
  <mediatype bind="mt1"/>
</upload>
```

Figure 6-5. Upload form control rendered with FormsPlayer

The XForms specification names a number of possible input sources:

file upload
> File upload is generally applicable, and works equally well for image, audio, text, data, and other files. Some of the smallest applications, perhaps phones, might not have a file system. But, in general, most devices capable of running XForms will have some notion of files suitable for uploading. HTML forms theoretically allowed multiple-file selection, but this never was widely implemented. In XForms, it's a single file only, though compound files (like .zip) are allowed.

scribble
> Scribble is applicable to images. One way to generate an image is to draw it; many electronics and department stores already have digitizer equipment in place to capture signatures for credit card processing. Barring some good excuse, implementations with specific pen hardware, including most handheld computers, are required to support a primitive drawing application, where the final result becomes the image data. Systems with conventional pointing devices, such as mice and trackballs, can also implement this technique.

acquire image
> Increasingly, computers of all sizes include image acquisition hardware, including digital cameras and scanners. When applicable, XForms can directly support these devices where an output form control requires image data.

record audio
> Another trend is to add audio recording hardware to all different kinds of devices. This adds another option for producing form data, when the desired format is audio.

record video
> Record video is straightforward. There aren't too many video forms in the world, at least not yet, but this didn't stop the designers of XForms form considering what the future might bring. This option allows digital video to become part of a form.

other possibilities
> For interoperability, the earlier options are all that have a reasonable chance of being implemented across a wide range of XForms devices, and even then you should carefully test your form on multiple devices. Input devices can change quickly, and the XForms specification gives general guidelines for future situations. For example, if 3D input devices were to become common, it should be possible to use them to enter form data. In controlled situations, custom-tailored input techniques could be used, such as a WYSIWYG text editor.

Control over what kinds of choices are presented falls to the `mediatype` attribute, which is a media (or MIME)-type string such as `image/png` or `application/zip`. If the specific subtype doesn't matter, it can be specified as the * character, as in `audio/*`. If this leads to a situation where no input is possible (for instance a request for `video/*` where there simply aren't any possible ways to generate a video file) the user has to be made aware of this problem rather than silently pretending it doesn't exist.

One unique aspect of this form control is that it can bind to the instance data in multiple places; for example, through the child elements `mediatype` and `filename`, each of which takes separate binding attributes. The actual media type and filename of the chosen data source, if known, are placed in the instance data. This is a one-way trip—these values are placed in the instance and not looked at again, and so are only for the benefit of the server application that processes the form data.

Only a binary-based type, such as `base64Binary` and `hexBinary`, or a derived datatype, can be used as the target of the uploaded data. Storing large amounts of binary data in XML poses some challenges, which are addressed in Chapter 8.

range

This form control wasn't present in HTML forms. It provides an intuitive way to enter a bounded value. The upper and lower bounds are set by the attributes start and end, respectively, and the suggested interval by the attribute step. Visually, this can be rendered as a slider, a rotary control, or a regular edit box with spin controls. Example 6-6 shows sample markup for a range control and Figure 6-6 shows the result in FormsPlayer.

Example 6-6. Sample markup for a range control

```
<range start="0" end="10" step="1" ref="quan" model="po">
  <label>Quantity</label>
</range>
```

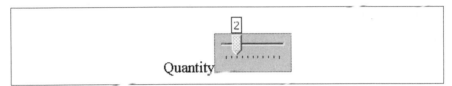

Figure 6-6. Range form control rendered with FormsPlayer

Only datatypes based on a particular list can be used with this form control: xs:duration, xs:date, xs:time, xs:dateTime, xs:gYearMonth, xs:gYear, xs:gMonthDay, xs:gDay, xs:gMonth, xs:float, xs:decimal, xs:double.

trigger

This form control is similar to the HTML element button and in fact was called that in earlier XForms drafts. The final name emphasizes that this form control really is a trigger for XForms Actions—a push button is just one possible rendering. Other possibilities include images, hyperlinks, mouse gestures, and voice activation. The rendering of this form control is often similar to the submit element. Example 6-7 shows sample markup for this control.

Example 6-7. Sample markup for a trigger control

```
<trigger>
  <label>Login</label>
  ...
</trigger>
```

Although this form control doesn't directly read or write form data, it takes binding attributes for the purpose of applying model item properties (relevant in particular) to the form control. Thus, it is possible to disable the trigger when needed.

This control has no restrictions on data binding.

submit

This form control is a specialization of trigger, with the effect of submitting the form. The submit parameters are taken from the element that matches the IDREF specified on the attribute submission. Example 6-8 shows sample markup for a submit control, and Figure 6-7 shows a rendering of it using Type.a Corp's Xero, available at *http://typeasoft.com/product/xero/*.

Example 6-8. Sample markup for the submit control

```
<submit submission="formdata">
  <label>Buy</label>
</submit>
```

Figure 6-7. Submit form control rendered with Xero

This form control has no restrictions on data binding.

select1

This form control represents selection from a list with the intent of enforcing the selection of exactly one item. In XForms, the list controls have a broader interpretation than in HTML forms. Any control that expresses the goal of picking things from a list, including conventional radio buttons and checkboxes fall into this category. Example 6-9 shows sample markup for a select1 control, and Figure 6-8 shows this control rendered with Ripcord Technology's nForms, available at *http://www.ripcord.co.nz/*.

Example 6-9. Sample markup for the select1 control

```
<select1 ref="cpu" appearance="full" accesskey="C">
  <label>CPU</label>
  <item>
    <label>Pentium 4 2.53Ghz - $220</label>
    <value>2.5</value>
  </item>
```

Example 6-9. Sample markup for the select1 control (continued)

```
  <item>
    <label>Pentium 4 2.8Ghz - $415</label>
    <value>2.8</value>
  </item>
  <item>
    <label>Pentium 4 3.06Ghz - $620</label>
    <value>3.0</value>
  </item>
</select1>
```

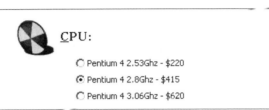

Figure 6-8. Select1 form control rendered with nForms

When the initial instance data contains a value (possibly even an empty value) that doesn't match any of the provided values, there will be no visible indication of what the selection is. Unlike the case with select, however, any user selection will replace the value in the instance data.

One special option with this form control is when the selection attribute is specified as open. This indicates that "free entry" is allowed, so that the user can either pick from the list or use input-style data entry to enter a value not originally in the list of items. The entered value is still subject to all the validation rules in XForms, including XML Schema datatype validation.

Some graphic designers are unnerved about the generality of this form control, and would prefer to explicitly indicate that they want, say, checkboxes instead of a drop-down list. The correct answer is, of course, to use CSS to style the control, as discussed in Chapter 9. In the general case, however, there's no guarantee that CSS (or any other style language) will be available at the point where the form is displayed. This is what the appearance attribute is all about. Because this request happens so often, the XForms specification gives some guidelines on how to indicate at a high level the desired rendering of the form control:

appearance="full"
> To always render all of the choices, a list of checkboxes or radiobuttons is used.

appearance="compact"
> To render a more compact list, a listbox that can have scroll bars to limit itself to a particular size, is used.

appearance="minimal"

To render a minimal list, as little as a single item is shown, with additional choices appearing, like a drop-down menu, upon request.

The configuration of select1, as shown previously in this section, binds to any XML Schema simpleContent; that is, to any kind of text whatsoever. Another configuration of the selection controls binds to an entire element plus content for the selection made.

select

This form control represents selection from a list with the intent of allowing nothing, one thing, or multiple things to be selected. It shares many common features with select1. Example 6-10 shows sample markup for a select control, and Figure 6-9 shows this form control rendered with Novell's XForms Technology Preview, available at *http://www.novell.com/xforms/*.

Example 6-10. Sample markup for the select control

```
<select ref="cctype">
  <label>List For Specifying All Card Types</label>
  <item>
    <label>Master Card</label>
    <value>MC</value>
  </item>
  <item>
    <label>Visa Card</label>
    <value>VI</value>
  </item>
  <item>
    <label>American Express</label>
    <value>AE</value>
  </item>
  <item>
    <label>Diners Club</label>
    <value>DC</value>
  </item>
</select>
```

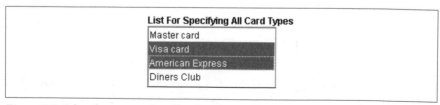

Figure 6-9. Select form control rendered with Novell XForms Technology Preview

The select form control is the most general kind of list, as it holds no restrictions on how many items the user may select from the list. When used as in the previous example, the resulting selections will be placed in an XML Schema space-separated list, and if any of the values contain whitespace characters, the list won't work as expected, because in the resulting confusion each space-separated token will be treated as a separate selection.

In this configuration, any initial data provided to the list needs to be a space-separated list. It is possible for the instance data to not match the values provided (through the initial value, or through direct manipulation of the instance data), in which case the form control is required to somehow notify the user that the data value is "out of range" (described more in Chapter 9). In fact, unless the form control has an "unselect all" affordance, such orphan selections will be more or less stuck in the instance data. Needless to say, this is bad practice in form design, and should be avoided.

Like select1, this form control allows authors a measure of control over the rendering through the appearance attribute.

The configuration of select, as shown previously in this section, binds to any XML Schema datatype that can hold a space-separated list. Ideally, this would be a list-derived datatype, but many built-in datatypes (such as string) work, too. The following section describes a configuration in which each selection binds to an individual element plus content.

Complex Lists

Lists as described in the previous two sections always bind to what XML Schema calls simpleContent, or text that (for example) could be in an attribute value. It's also possible to configure a select or select1 so that each selected item corresponds to an element in the instance data, and thus changing the selection has the effect of changing the instance data at a structural level.

Before describing how this works, it's necessary to take a brief diversion to see how lists can get their set of possible selections from instance data rather than hard-coded values as shown previously. Instead of individual item elements, it is possible for list controls to obtain the list of things from which to select through an itemset element, which selects multiple instance data nodes and produces a potential selection out of each. This example uses multiple XForms Models:

```
<xforms:model id="list_items">
  <xforms:instance>
    <options>
      <email desc="work address">mdubinko@example.info</email>
```

```
      <email desc="home address">mdubinko@example.org</email>
      <email desc="alternate address">nospam@example.net</email>
    </options>
  </xforms:instance>
<xforms:model>

...

<xforms:model id="form_data">
  <xforms:instance>
    <user_selection/>
  </xforms:instance>
</xforms:model>

...

<xforms:select ref="." model="form_data">
  <xforms:label>Send a copy to the following email addresses</xforms:
        label<xforms:itemset nodeset="email" model="list_items">
    <xforms:label><xforms:output value="concat('Your ', @desc)"/></xforms:
label>
    <xforms:value ref="."/>
  </xforms:itemset>
</xforms:select>
```

The single itemset element is responsible for all of the list choices. In this example, that's three items since the nodeset="email" attribute selects three nodes from the XForms Model list_items. For each node, the child elements of itemset are evaluated in turn, with the node in question as the context node. Thus, the expression concat('Your ', @desc) produces three different labels, which happen to match the labels on the earlier select example. Similarly, the value elements are evaluated and converted into text strings that also match the earlier example.

For this to work, the node-set returned by the expression on the nodeset attribute must be *homogeneous*, that is:

- All the nodes must be element nodes, and have the same parent element node.
- All the nodes must have the same name, including the namespace.
- All the nodes must be contiguous; there must not be any other nodes in-between, so, for instance, the following-node axis in XPath would select every node with no gaps.

The copy element serves the same purpose as the value element, except that instead of producing a text value to insert into the instance data, it does a "deep copy," including attributes, text, and child elements. Thus, the arrangement of the instance data for the list depends on whether it uses value or copy elements. With the first two items selected, the respective instance data would look like:

```
Instance data with <value>:
<user_selection>mdubinko@example.info mdubinko@example.org</user_selection>
```

```
Instance data with <copy>:
<user_selection>
  <email desc="work address">mdubinko@example.info</email>
  <email desc="home address">mdubinko@example.org</email>
</user_selection>
```

Note that in the second case, even the desc attribute is copied.

Overall, the behavior of itemset is very similar to repeat, which is discussed in "Repeating Line Items," later in this chapter.

Common Markup

There are elements and attributes that appear on many form controls.

Labels

Labels on form controls are incredibly useful. In conventional paper forms, labels are nearly always present. One problem with previous generations of web forms, however, was that authors tended to not use explicit labels, instead including text that happened to be visually nearby the form control—a practice that makes life more difficult for non-visual users. XForms attacks this problem at the foundation by making the label element *required*.

The content of the label can be text, markup (including images) from the host language, or an output form control. Further, the label can be from an external file (through the src attribute), or text taken from instance data (through the single node binding attributes).

Styling a label independently from the form control poses a unique twist, since styles will normally inherit to child elements. Chapter 9 describes the advances in CSS that deal with this challenge.

help, hint, and alert

Another form design problem is ensuring that users have the correct expectations for the kind of data they are asked to enter. In XForms, every form control can have a help element, which contains a message that's provided upon an explicit request (such as pushing the Help or F1 key). The help message is delivered in a way that is equivalent to a modeless message, as discussed at Chapter 7. Likewise, form controls can have a hint element, which contains a message that's shown at the discretion of the XForms Processor, for instance, if the user hovers the mouse over a form control for more than a given amount of time. The hint message is equivalent to an ephemeral message, as discussed in Chapter 7.

A third kind of element, alert, contains a message to be shown to the user when an error condition (like a form control failing validation) happens. Unlike help and hint, there's no universal way to deliver alert information to the user. This is because when the user tries to submit, there could potentially be several validation errors that come to light at the same time, and it may be advantageous to combine several messages into one.

Like label, these elements can also get their contents from an external source (e.g., through the src attribute), or from the instance data (e.g., through ref and the other single-node binding attributes).

Navigation order

A critical, but too often overlooked, part of a form design is configuring the navigation order. A Tab or Next key is a standard part of nearly every device these days, and it's important that the default path through a form makes life easier for the form users. The actual mechanism for navigation depends on the host language, although XForms defines a suggested minimum level of performance, based on an attribute that would appear on every form control.

The default rules for determining the navigation order are essentially unchanged from HTML forms: each control can have an attribute named navindex, which holds a number between 0 and 32767. (For programming geeks, this upper limit is the largest number that a signed 16-bit integer can hold.) The navigation order starts with 1 and proceeds to progressively higher numbers, and finishes with form controls that don't specify navindex (or equivalently, specify it as 0). In the case of a tie, the navigation follows the order that the form controls appear in the document. Groups, switches, and repeats form local navigation units, which means that all the form controls in that group will be navigated, following the same rules here, before the focus proceeds to other controls outside the group.

Through relevant (see Chapter 5), it's possible to have form controls that are no longer effectively part of the navigation sequence. The XForms specification states that even when this is the case, those form controls still have a relative order assigned, even though they are skipped. This means that should the form control become relevant, it will find itself at the right place in the navigation order.

XForms doesn't define what happens when either end of the navigation order is reached, though browsers typically cycle back to the other end of the form, with a few stops in between for the browser itself. The host language also might contain various object that can be part of the navigation order. By giving the host language ultimate control, the overall sequence can be one that makes sense in the full context of the document.

Keyboard shortcuts

On shorter forms, standard navigation is usually sufficient. Longer or more complex forms, however, are different story. A small thing like a quick keyboard shortcut to get to a form control can dramatically improve the usability of a form. Like navigation order, keyboard shortcuts fall into the domain of the host language. One common approach is to use an attribute named accesskey, which contains a character that is used with a platform-specific modifier key (typically the Alt key on Windows and Linux, and the Control key on Mac) to set focus quickly to a particular form control.

A couple of warnings are in order: browsers usually reserve a fair number of keyboard shortcuts for themselves, so try to pick characters that aren't already in use. Some devices, phones in particular, might not have individual letter keys, so a numeric access key might be the best way to go.

You should always document within the form what the access keys are—this will help the form users to learn about the shortcuts.

Coarse-grained appearance

The section on select discussed the appearance attribute and gave some specific examples from the XForms specification. Actually, the appearance attribute is present on all form controls, and can give general guidelines on the kind of appearance you are aiming for as a form designer.

Of course, for detailed control, you'll need CSS (see Chapter 9) or some other style sheet language.

Input mode

Before I was exposed to the worldly ways of global computing, I had often pondered idly about how keyboards work for languages with thousands of characters. Just how many keys are on those kinds of keyboards, anyway? The problem of entering a language or script on a different keyboard than one for the native language is accomplished by a piece of software called an Input Method Editor, or IME. Through the inputmode attribute, XForms allows form controls that accept direct keyboard input to give a hint for the appropriate IME to switch to when first entering the form control. The content of this attribute is a space separated list of tokens, which fall into three categories: script tokens (see Table 6-1), modifier tokens (see Table 6-2), and URIs. As a general catch-all, any token not already in the list can be assigned a URI and used like any other token in the inputmode attribute.

Table 6-1. Script tokens

arabic	armenian
bengali	bopomofo
braille	buhid
canadianAboriginal	cherokee
cyrillic	deseret
devanagari	ethiopic
georgian	greek
gothic	gujarati
gurmukhi	han
hangul	hanja
hanunoo	hebrew
hiragana	ipa (International Phonetic Alphabet)
kanji	kannada
katakana	khmer
lao	latin
malayalam	math (mathematical symbols)
mongolian	myanmar
ogham	oldItalic
oriya	runic
simplifiedHanzi	sinhala
syriac	tagalog
tagbanwa	tamil
telugu	thaana
thai	tibetan
traditionalHanzi	user (Special value denoting the 'native' input mode of the user)
yi	

Table 6-2. Modifier tokens

lowerCase	upperCase
titleCase	startUpper
digits	symbols
predictOn	predictOff
halfWidth	

Upon seeing the lists in Tables 6-1 and 6-2, most users wonder why so many choices were included. Since the values are only hints, there's no additional cost associated with a long list, and the additional values might help certain classes of users. The list of the modifiers in Table 6-2 is more generally useful, as it includes options for automatically controlling the case of input text, and other options that are especially useful for phone keypads, such as predictive text or digit-only mode.

Event handlers

Additional child elements of each form control, as well as list items, can contain event handlers, as discussed in Chapter 7.

Interaction with Instance Data

Form controls transform the user input into either a string of characters (called simpleContent) or child elements. In XML, character data can occur in many ways, including attributes, element content, comments, processing instructions, and so on. For the most part, XForms interacts intuitively with XML.

When bound to an attribute or an element with text-only content, the mapping is straightforward: it uses the attribute value or the text child node of the attribute:

```
ref="/element"
<element>form data</element>

ref="/element/text( )"
<element>form data</element> (equivalent to direct element reference)

ref="/element/@attribute"
<element attribute="form data"/>
```

For these purposes, an empty element (<element/>) is treated as a zero-length string.

Comments and processing instructions are straightforward: don't do it. To encourage authors to keep important form data in elements and attributes, XForms leaves the binding undefined for comments and processing instructions (if these exist in the initial instance data, they will be passed through unchanged, so this admonition applies only to their use in storing form data).

It gets more complicated when mixed content enters the picture. When confronted with this situation, a new text node will be created as the first child of the target element, which usually isn't the intended effect. Thus, mixed content isn't supported in off-the-shelf XForms 1.0, though some proposed extensions enable the common case of XHTML.

Generally, elements that contain other elements or a combination of text and elements shouldn't be used as an endpoint for form data.

Incremental

The remaining question concerns when the update happens. Does an `input` form control cause a change in the instance data, with the associated flurry of recalculation activity, on a per-keystroke basis? Or does no update happen until the user navigates away, as is the case in current HTML forms?

The answer is that an attribute, named `incremental`, controls this behavior. A setting of `false` causes the update, with the `xforms-value-changed` notification event, to occur only when the user navigates away. This is the default setting for `input`, `secret`, `textarea`, `range`, and `upload`. However, when the attribute value is `true`, updates and additional `xforms-value-changed` events happen more frequently, although the specification doesn't go as far as saying "per keystroke." In fact, having a keyboard isn't a requirement to run XForms. More frequent updates are the default for `select` and `select1`.

Grouping

Groups make possible a number of conveniences, but also have a functional aspect. In nearly every respect, a group is another kind of form control, and thus model item properties such as `relevant` and `required` can apply to a group, and override those properties on any contained form controls. This is most useful when an entire section of a form needs to change based on some condition in the instance data. The `switch` element can provide similar functionality, though only based on explicit events to toggle one of several alternatives into view. The group approach works better when the dynamic behavior desired relates directly to the instance data.

Groups can also help authors with a couple of shortcuts:

- The group element can be a convenient place to declare the XForms Namespace as the default namespace, to reduce the clutter of repeated prefixes or additional declarations. In languages like XHTML 2.0 that import the XForms elements into a common namespace, this is less of an issue.

- Binding attributes can be declared, to set a new context node for any binding expressions that occur within the group. For example, if all the grouped form controls are to reference instance data underneath `my:Envelope/my:ExcessivelyNestedElement`, that portion of the XPath can be written only once on the group element, like this:

```
<xforms:group ref="my:Envelope/my:ExcessivelyNestedElement">
  <xforms:input ref="my:Leaf">
  ...
</xforms:group>
```

In the example, the grouped input form control is spared from having to fully spell out the XPath expression to the desired node, which would be `my:Envelope/my:ExcessivelyNestedElement/my:Leaf`. When groups contain multiple form controls, the savings gained by avoiding needless repetition can be substantial.

Dynamic Presentation

For years now, developers have used complicated scripting and other desperate measures to create "dynamic forms." For instance, one commercial product I worked on (see *http://www.Cardiff.com/LiquidOffice*) used HTML divs to represent individual "pages" of a multi-page form, with script to swap the current page. Using XForms, the same effect can be accomplished declaratively.

switch and case

The `switch` element is a container for case elements, usually two or more. At any given time, the contents of exactly one of the cases will be rendered in the final document, and the rest of the cases will be suppressed. One use of this is to provide tabbed interfaces, as Figure 6-10 shows, rendered with the open source Chiba project, available at *http://chiba.sourceforge.net*.

One immediate use of this feature is to provide a text message that only appears to non-XForms compatible browsers, by including a message in a case that gets hidden before the form displays. If XForms processing doesn't happen, then the initial message remains.

```
<model>
  <toggle ev:event="xforms-ready" case="go">
  ...
</model>

<switch>
  <case id="default_message">You are using a browser that doesn't support
XForms</case>
  <case id="go">...</case>
</switch>
```

More generally, `switch` is useful for simulating pages, showing and hiding portions of the form, and enhancing the usability of forms by suppressing parts that don't matter at a given moment.

Each case element has a `selected` attribute, defaulted if necessary, that is visible to the host document, including DOM and CSS interfaces. Additionally, `xforms-select` and `xforms-deselect` events are dispatched to the

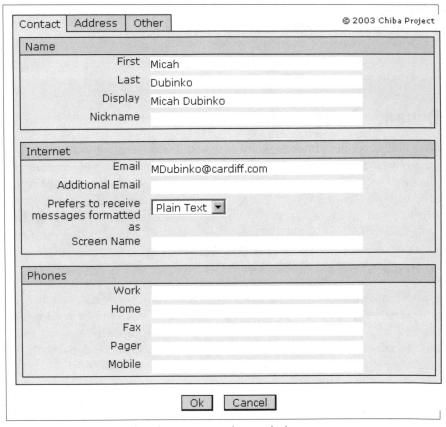

Figure 6-10. Tabbed interface demonstrating the switch element

individual cases, allowing event handlers to respond in a centralized manner to changes.

The actual switch is accomplished by an XForms Action named toggle, which takes a parameter of an IDREF that refers to the particular case that will become active.

Repeating Line Items

One of the most sorely missed features in HTML forms comes by many names: tables, grid controls, or line items. The basic concept is that many forms in common use don't fit in well with a flat list of form controls. Figure 6-11 shows one embodiment of this, rendered in the X-Smiles browser.

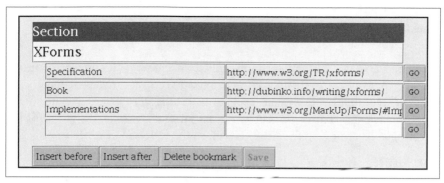

Figure 6-11. Repeating line items in X-Smiles

Another common scenario is a purchase order, with repeating lines, each containing quantity, description, price, and computed extended price.

repeat

The primary means of accomplishing this in XForms is the repeat element, which operates over homogeneous collections, the same as itemset, described earlier. The nodeset attribute of repeat selects a number of nodes, and the contents of the element, both from XForms and from the host language, are effectively repeated once for each resulting node. One way to think of this is to "unroll" the repeat, so that the following:

```
<repeat nodeset="item">
  <input ref="@quantity" .../>
</repeat>
```

has a similar effect, when the nodeset returns three item nodes, to:

```
<input ref="item[1]/@quantity" .../>
<input ref="item[2]/@quantity" .../>
<input ref="item[3]/@quantity" .../>
```

The main difference between a repeat element and unrolled syntax (besides convenience) is how the result is presented to the user. The repeat version makes it possible to show more items in a limited space, as in the case of scroll bars. Attributes of repeat further refine this by specifying how the initial appearance should be:

startindex
Specifies what the initial visible position should be, typically 1.

number
Specifies how many items should be initially visible. If this number is smaller than the number of nodes selected, then typically scroll bars will result.

Items can be added and removed from repeat with the XForms Actions insert and delete, which are given as examples here and described fully in chapter Chapter 7.

Every repeat has a current position, called an *index*. The concept of index extends the concept of focus, so that if a form control in a repeat has focus, then the item that contains that form control is the current index. The XPath function index( ) returns the current index of any repeat. This is useful for inserting at or removing the current item, as the following example shows:

```
<model>
  <instance>
    <items xmlns="">
      <item quantity="1" price="2.34"/>
    </items>
  </instance>
</model>
...
<repeat nodeset="items/item" id="r1">
  <input ref="@quantity" .../>
  <output ref="@price" .../>
</repeat>

<!-- insert just after the index item -->
<trigger>
  <label>Insert</label>
  <insert nodeset="/items/item" at="index('r1')" position="after"/>
  <setvalue ref="/items/item[index('r1')]/@quantity">0</quantity>
  <setvalue ref="/items/item[index('r1')]/@price">0.00</setvalue>
</trigger>

<!-- delete the index item -->
<trigger>
  <label>Delete</label>
  <delete ev:event="DOMActivate" nodeset="/items/item" at="index('r1')"/>
</trigger>
```

Newly inserted items are copied exactly from the last item in the repeat node-set. If the copied values aren't suitable, they can be overridden with setvalue, as in this example.

Attribute Syntax

One problem that arises with the repeat element is that a host language might not be able to add arbitrary elements where a repeating structure is needed. A prime example of this is HTML table. It would be natural to express a repeating sequence as table rows or table cells (or a nested repeat with both). The problem with that is that if XHTML allowed repeat in the content model of table or tr, that would open the floodgates and allow all kinds of non-table related markup. For cases like these, the XForms specification defines special attributes that can be included in a host language, if needed. The attributes all share the same prefix: repeat-nodeset, repeat-model, repeat-bind, repeat-startindex, and repeat-number. The first three of these work just like the unprefixed node-set binding attributes, and the last two work just like the corresponding attributes on repeat. The table example in XHTML, with repeating table rows, looks like this:

```
<table repeat-nodeset="item">
  <tr>
    <td><output ref="@quantity" .../></td>
    <td><output ref="@price" .../></td>
  </tr>
</table>
```

Attribute-style repeat is identical to element-style repeat, other than the surface syntax. The part that gets repeated is the contents of the element holding the special repeat attributes.

CHAPTER 7
Actions and Events

"While we are free to choose our actions, we are not free to choose the consequences of our actions."
—Stephen Covey

"We are not ready for any unforeseen event that may or may not occur."
—Dan Quayle

Scripting. It sounds good, at first. With a quick hack, it can cure every problem you throw at it. It's seductive. The problem is, a couple of months later, when you need to fix a bug or add another feature, you can't remember what the script was supposed to do, and you spend a week reverse engineering the whole system. And you'll do it again a few months later. And again, and again. The major problem with script is that even though it's easy to get started with, it's expensive to maintain. If you don't believe it, try debugging someone *else's* script some time.

There are other problems with scripting as well. Scripts are usually biased towards a visual platform, which means that accessibility aids, or even just regular users with an eyes-free browser, will tend to have trouble with scripting. For the foreseeable future, security-conscious users will have scripting disabled in their browsers.

The answer is to identify areas where scripting is most commonly needed, and create declarative replacements, which is exactly what XForms accomplishes. The core technology that makes this possible is called XML Events.

XML Events

An event, as far as XForms is concerned, is a data structure that gets passed around to certain interfaces, called event listeners. The Document Object

Model (DOM) Level 2 Events specification spells out how events work. The latter part of this chapter describes specific events that are useful in XForms authoring.

Each event has a target element, which represents the point where the main action is happening, from the viewpoint of a particular event. Each event also can have a default action that is effectively triggered by the event. For example, an xforms-focus event will have a form control element as a target and a default action of changing the active focus. DOM Level 2 includes a method to configure an observer, which can take a specific action in response to an event, possibly in lieu of the default action. The most common case is for the observer to attach directly to the target element.

In some cases, however, an observer would like to have broader access to events, for instance to all xforms-focus events for all form controls. In this scenario, the observer is farther downstream from the event target. DOM Level 2 Events define how events "propagate" (or flow) through the DOM, as shown in Figure 7-1.

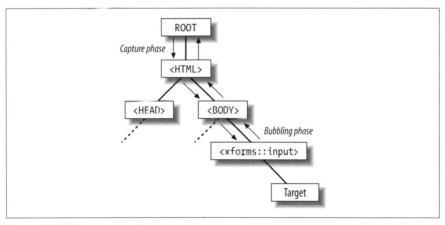

Figure 7-1. Event propagation

Event propagation is divided into two phases: capture and bubbling. Capture occurs first, as the DOM root node is given the option to observe the event, then additional nodes following the path from the root to the target element. Any listener has the ability to end the propagation, or to prevent the default action of the event. After reaching the target (and giving observers there a change to handle the event), the event reverses course and makes its way back to the root, in a process called bubbling. If the event finishes this journey without being cancelled, the default action happens as long as no listeners have signaled to block the default action.

The Old Way

In the design of HTML forms, script is used whenever some specific action is needed. For example, a form might have a button that copies values from a "ship to" section onto a "bill to" section. In HTML forms plus script, the following code would accomplish this:

```
<script type="text/javascript"> <!--

function copyAddresses( ) {
  var frm = document.forms[0];
  frm.shipAddr.value = frm.billAddr.value;
  frm.shipCity.value = frm.billCity.value;
  frm.shipProv.value = frm.billProv.value;
  frm.shipPostCode.value = frm.billPostCode.value;
}
--> </script>
```

This code simply copies form values from one control to another. It would then be activated by a button, with an event-specific attribute, specified like this:

```
<input type="button" id="cp" value="Copy values" onclick="copyAddresses( )"/>
```

In terms of DOM Level 2 Events, this represents a registration of an observer on the input element, watching for the DOM click event at the target, and handling the event by calling a short script. As a result, the script in the onclick attribute will get called when the user clicks on the button.

Note that a minor leap of faith is required by the browser to interpret the contents of the onclick attribute as JavaScript—in principle, any scripting language could be used, and a special meta tag would be needed to specify which scripting language is truly in use in the event attributes. (In practice, nobody actually does this, and browsers just muddle through, making essentially an educated guess, almost always JavaScript.) To recap the disadvantages of this approach:

- A special hardwired attribute, in this case onclick, is needed. This is inflexible and clutters the language.
- Script is difficult to maintain, especially when bits of script are scattered throughout the document.
- This won't work in browsers that don't support scripting.

XML Events solves all of these problems by specifying a better way to observe and, ultimately, handle events.

Listeners, Observers, and Handlers

XML Events provides an element-based syntax for DOM Level 2 events. It defines a listener element that, even though not directly used in XForms, is still worth examining. This element has eight attributes defined:

event

> This attribute specifies the name of the attribute to be observed. Event names are defined in DOM Level 2 Events (for general-purpose events) and in XForms, as in Chapter 7.

observer

> This attribute specifies, by an IDREF, the element to which the observer is to be attached.

target

> This attribute specifies, by an IDREF, the desired target element for which to observe events. When this attribute is specified, events that would otherwise register will be ignored if the target doesn't match.

handler

> This attribute specifies, by a URI reference, the desired handler for the event. XForms defines a number of handlers, covered in the next section. Note that to specify an element through a URI reference, a so-called "fragment identifier" beginning with the # character has to be used; for example, "#handler".

phase

> This attribute specifies the DOM Level 2 Events phase in which the observer is to be active. Note that a single observer can't look for both the capture and bubbling phases. The possible values for this attribute are the self-explanatory capture, or default, which covers both the target and the bubbling phase.

propagate

> This attribute determines whether the event will continue to propagate. The possible values for this attribute are stop or continue (the default).

defaultAction

> This attribute determines whether the default action will be activated for an event. The possible values are cancel and perform (the default). If any observer at any point indicates cancel, then the default processing will not occur. Some events aren't cancellable, and so ignore this attribute.

The specification also calls for an id attribute to be declared by the host language. If the listener element was used in XHTML, it might look like the following.

```
<head>
  <listener event="click" observer="btn" handler="#id_of_handler"/>
  ...
</head>
```

While these attributes map directly to equivalent concepts in DOM Level 2 Events, it can be cumbersome to provide an extra element with extra attributes. To accommodate for this, the XML Events specification contains a few shortcuts, based on namespaced or global attributes. These attributes can be placed directly on the observer element:

```
<body>
  ...
  <input type="button" ev:event="click" ev:handler="#id_of_handler"/>
  ...
</body>
```

Alternatively, the attributes can be placed on the handler element:

```
<head>
  <script type="text/javascript" ev:event="click" ev:observer="btn">...</
script>
  ...
</head>
```

This final technique is used extensively in XForms.

Declarative Actions, Displacing Script

The example in the previous section had a script element that was designated as a "handler." What is the source of such handlers?

Handlers can come from two sources. XForms defines a number of handlers, called XForms Actions, discussed below. Additionally, the host language can define handlers, as is the case with script.

With XForms Actions, the earlier example can be done without any script at all, like this:

```
<trigger>
  <label>Copy values</label>
  <action ev:event="DOMActivate">
    <setvalue ref="Shipping/Addr" value="../Billing/Addr"/>
    <setvalue ref="Shipping/City" value="../Billing/City"/>
    <setvalue ref="Shipping/Prov" value="../Billing/Prov"/>
    <setvalue ref="Shiping/PostCode" value="../Billing/PostCode"/>
  </action>
</trigger>
```

XForms Actions

The following sections describe all of the XForms Actions defined in XForms. Any of the following can be invoked in such a way that the processing described for the element happens in response to a given event.

message

This action directs a message to the user, with various possible levels of intrusiveness, based on the required attribute level. In scripting, this effect is commonly implemented with the alert( ) function, which is the most intrusive technique, since it is modal, and prevents any further action until the user dismisses the message. XForms enables friendlier (and less visual-centric) messages: *modeless*, which doesn't interfere with the rest of the form, but sticks around until dismissed; and *ephemeral*, a fleeting, goes-away-by-itself message, such as a tool tip or brief status bar message.

Figure 7-2 shows visual representations of various messages.

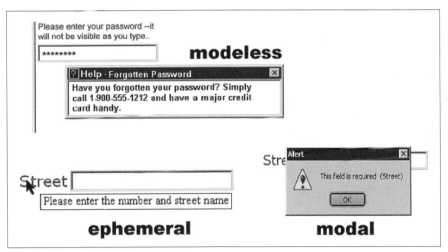

Figure 7-2. XForms Action: message

The general concept of various levels of intrusiveness applies well to non-visual designs, too; for example, the difference between an insistent voice prompt that requires acknowledgement versus a one-time message.

Typically, the content of the message element is the message to be rendered. Like other XForms elements, the content can also come from the instance data (from binding attributes) or from an external file (from linking attributes). Only a single source is ever used; the order of preference is: binding attributes, linking attributes, inline text, as shown next.

```
<message level="ephemeral" ev:event="DOMFocusIn">Produced by PBP</message>
<message level="modeless" model="messages" ref="instructions/part3"
            ev:event="xforms-help"/>
<message level="modal" src="important.html" ev:event="DOMActivate">
```

setvalue

Binding attributes on this element select the location in the instance data to receive the value, which is always simpleContent. Note that XForms doesn't include a way to arbitrarily alter complexContent through XForms Actions, though the insert and delete actions can to a limited extent.

Another job commonly reserved for scripting is to set values in the form, as shown in the earlier example in this chapter. This action can set the value of an attribute node or an element's text node, to either a fixed value or the result of evaluating XPath.

The value to place in the instance is either an XPath expression, contained in the value attribute, or literal text as the content of the element. If both should happen to be present, the evaluated XPath is used.

Clearing a value is the same as setting a zero-length string—in other words, neither a value attribute nor element content.

setvalue can be useful in several contexts, as shown here:

```
<!-- on initialize, set a value of "0" -->
<setvalue bind="frequency" ev:event="xforms-ready">0</setvalue>
...
<!-- on initialize, copy the billing address to the shipping address -->
<setvalue ref="Shipping/Addr" value="../Billing/Addr"
            ev:event="xforms-ready"/>
...
<!-- clear a value when an Insert happens -->
<setvalue bind="phone_num" ev:event="xforms-insert"/>
```

setfocus

This action redirects the focus to a different form control. An attribute named control holds an IDREF of the form control that will get focus.

In effect, this action does nothing more than dispatch an xforms-focus event to the form control indicated. It can be used like this:

```
<setfocus control="Address_1" ev:event="xforms-ready"/>
```

send

This action invokes submission of a form. A required attribute submission holds an IDREF to a submission element that contains the details of what and how to submit.

The effect is the same as dispatching an xforms-submit event to the submission element indicated. Details of submit options are discussed in Chapter 8.

```
<send submission="submis3" ev:event="DOMActivate"/>
```

reset

A reset control is probably the most overused form control on the web. (This is why XForms doesn't define a reset control) Still, in the right circumstances, it's necessary to reset a form, which is what this action does. It takes an attribute model, which contains the IDREF of the model element that will be reset.

The *reset condition* is defined as the state the instance data was in immediately after the xforms-ready event was dispatched. reset can be used like this:

```
<reset model="weather" ev:event="DOMActivate"/>
```

load

This action traverses a link, possibly in a new window (or browsing context for non-visual devices), possibly replacing the active form. The optional attribute show, which can have a value of either "new" or "replace", determines the behavior.

The URL that the link goes to can either be specified in the resource attribute, or it can be in the instance data, pointed to by binding attributes (bind, or ref optionally with model).

 Never include both linking attributes and a resource attribute since having both is an invalid combination, that results in the load action having no effect at all.

Two ways to use the load action are like this:

```
<load resource="http://www.example.com" ev:event="DOMActivate"
show="replace"/>
<load ref="linktable/nextpage" ev:event="DOMFocusOut" show="new"/>
```

toggle

This action works with a switch element, selecting by IDREF a particular *case* within. The selected case is rendered, while all other cases are not. The ability to show and hide sections is a handy way to implement a "multiple page" form, which guides the user through one section at a time. It's also useful within a page, to set up wizard-like sequences, or just to hide entire sections of the form that aren't needed at the moment.

Each *case* contains a selected attribute, which stays in sync, so that at any given time one and only one of the cases in a switch will have selected="true". In fact, in systems that support CSS2 selectors, one possible implementation is with the rule case[selected="false"] { display: none }.

The toggle action is used like this:

```
<toggle case="summary" ev:event="DOMActivate"/>
```

insert

This action works within a node-set, by constructing new nodes based on a template. The immediate problem with this approach is that if there are no nodes present in the repeating set (as can happen after invoking the delete action), what template can be used to copy from? The answer depends on the way instance data is constructed in XForms: as a separate in-memory representation. The initial instance data, as it appears inside the instance element in the containing document (or in an external linked file) doesn't change as the instance data changes through all the various interactions defined by XForms. Thus, the initial instance data is defined as the source of the template to be copied, even though it makes for some awkward terminology to explain how it works.

The main attributes that control the operation of this element are:

single-node binding attributes
> These attribute or attributes select a node-set, which matches the node-set selected by a repeat set.

at
> This attribute selects the location within the node-set where the inserted element node will appear. Generally, it is one of three possibilities:

- To insert a new repeat item at the beginning, at="1".
- To insert a new repeat item at the end, at="last( )".
- To insert a new repeat item at the current index, at="index('id_of_repeat')" (where id_of_repeat represents the IDREF of the <repeat> element).

position
> This attribute is required, and must be either "before" or "after"—where to insert the new node relative to the node selected by at.

The at attribute is evaluated as an XPath number, which creates a few edge cases that need to be addressed:

- Negative or zero results are treated like "1".
- Results larger than the size of the node-set, or that can't be interpreted as a number at all, are treated like "last( )".
- Fractional results are treated as if passed through a call to the XPath core function round( ), so that "1.5" becomes 2.

Once the location for the new node is determined, a new element node is manufactured by parsing the corresponding portion of the initial instance data, taking the final node present, which is deep copied into the instance data. This example demonstrates:

```
<model>
  <instance>
    <order xmlns="">
      <items>
        <item price="1.00"/>
        <item price="2.00"/>
        <item price="3.00"/>
      </items>
    </order>
  </instance>
</model>
...
<repeat id="repeat_id" nodeset="order/items/item">
  <input ref="@price">
    <label>Price</label>
  </input>
</repeat>
...
<trigger>
  <label>Insert a new item after the current one</label>
  <action ev:event="DOMActivate">
    <insert nodeset="/order/items/item" at="index('repeat_id')"
position="after"/>
    <setvalue ref="/order/items/item[index('lineset')]/@price"/>
  </action>
</trigger>
```

In this example, every time an insert action happens, the element node that gets copied is the one that reads <item price="3.00"/>, being the final member of the repeat set in the initial instance data. This is true no matter what insertions or deletions happen to the instance data. This example also shows following an insert with a setvalue, to give the newly-inserted node a desired value (in this case, empty).

Another question that comes up is what model item properties apply to the newly-inserted nodes. All bind expressions that point into the repeat set are reevaluated, so the model item properties can be applied equally to the new nodes.

As a typical result of insert, a new repeating item will be rendered in the user interface. The newly-inserted repeat item also becomes the repeat index, effectively giving focus to the new content.

delete

This action is the counterpart of insert—it removes nodes from the instance data. Without the issues of copying nodes from a template, the overall operation of this element is much simpler.

This element also has an attribute named at, which operates the same way as insert. It identifies an element node that is removed, along with any associated nodes (content text nodes, child element nodes, attribute nodes, and so on). The corresponding user interface for the repeat will also adjust to the now smaller repeat set.

This example continues the example in the previous section:

```
<trigger>
  <label>Remove current item</label>
  <delete ev:event="activate" nodeset="/order/items/item"
   at="index('repeat_id')"/>
</trigger>
```

setindex

Every repeat set keeps track of a current item, similar to a database cursor. The official term for this is the *index*. The index item behaves for multiple form controls much as a focus behaves for single form controls. In fact, setting the focus to a form control in a repeat set also adjusts the index to that spot. This action explicitly changes the index.

Two attributes control the behavior of this element: repeat, which takes an IDREF of a repeat set, and index, which takes an XPath expression that evaluates to a number, just as the as attribute on insert and delete.

setindex is used like this:

```
<setindex repeat="repeat_id" index="1" ev:event="xforms-ready"/>
```

revalidate, recalculate, refresh, and rebuild

XForms keeps track of computational dependencies, like a spreadsheet, so that any chained calculations properly resolve themselves in the face of changes. This action explicitly invokes a rebuilding of the dependencies, and is almost never needed.

These four actions trigger the processing involved with revalidation, recalculation, refresh, and rebuilding dependencies, respectively. Under normal conditions, all of these activities take place automatically, and form authors don't even need to consider these events or actions.

The primary exception, however, is on limited platforms where any of these activities might be expensive, in terms of processing or perceived user delay. When that's the case, it's not desirable for these events to happen automatically. Instead, users will want to have greater control over exactly when such things happen. This is similar to the concept of spreadsheets that have an option to turn off automatic recalculation.

To do this in XForms is a two-step process. First, an observer needs to be set up to cancel all automatically generated events for the expensive process (recalculation in this example). That step, by itself, will result in the recalculation never happening, which doesn't work so well. So the second step is to provide an option for the user to manually fire off a recalculate. This example shows both aspects:

```
<model ev:event="xforms-recalculate" ev:defaultAction="cancel">
...
<trigger>
  <label>Recalculate now</label>
  <recalculate ev:event="DOMActivate"/>
</trigger>
```

Note that this works because the recalculate action directly invokes the processing, without the intervening event flow (which would get cancelled by the observer on model anyway).

dispatch

This action dispatches any event to any element. In a sense, this is the most powerful XForms Action since, through events, nearly anything can be done.

This element contains four special attributes. The two required attributes are name, which names the event, and target, which holds the IDREF of the element that will be the target of the event. Two other optional attributes (bubbles and cancelable) specify whether the event can bubble or be cancelled, though all the predefined events have their own specification and can't be overridden.

An advanced technique is to create custom events, which can be dispatched and observed to accomplish specific behaviors, like this:

```
<dispatch name="xforms-refresh" target="model3" ev:event="DOMActivate"/>
<dispatch name="show-easter-egg" target="listener9" cancelable="false"
          ev:event="my-custom-evt"/>
```

action

This element is a wrapper for other XForms Actions. It contains child elements that are executed in sequence.

action can be used like this:

```
<action ev:event="DOMActivate">
  <setvalue ref="email/contact" value="email/admin"/>
  <message level="ephemeral">Synchronized email addresses</message>
</action>
```

One concept that comes into play in more advanced XForms scenarios is what the specification calls "deferred updates." This feature is intended to reduce the potentially expensive computation that can occur through an XForms Action, as changes to the instance data can trigger a display refresh, a recalculation, a revalidation, or a reconstruction of the dependencies.

Deferred updates occur only through the action container element. It can be thought of as a switch that temporarily turns off the expensive processing, handles the child elements, and then catches up on any processing that still needs to be done. In this way, for instance, a series of insert actions, when placed inside an action element, wouldn't require a full recalculation for each insert—just one to ensure consistency at the end.

Deferred updates apply to insert, delete, and setvalue.

Because of the way the XML Events defaulting works, placing ev:event attributes on XForms Action elements inside action will have no effect. Instead, the attribute should be placed on the action element itself—the XForms Actions as child elements will still run within the context of the action.

XForms Events

The XML Events specification provides a clean declarative way to call out actions that should be performed under certain conditions. Under what conditions, exactly? That depends on a processing model—including the definition of what events are involved, and when they become active.

At the time of this writing, the topic of XML processing models was still under fervent discussion in various pockets of standards activity, with no obvious end in sight. Each XML specification contains details of its own self-contained processing model, but nowhere is there a description of how different specifications interact or relate to one another. XForms is no different.

An entire chapter in the XForms specification is devoted to the processing model. Much of this material, however, is mainly of interest to programmers who happen to be implementing an XForms support in some product. For form authors, a simpler view is possible.

Stages of XForms Processing

The life-cycle of an XForms processor can be divided into several categories, which is a useful viewpoint for a form author. By scrutinizing what you want to accomplish, you can narrow down the potentially huge list of events to a more manageable list. Figure 7-3 shows the stages of XForms processing.

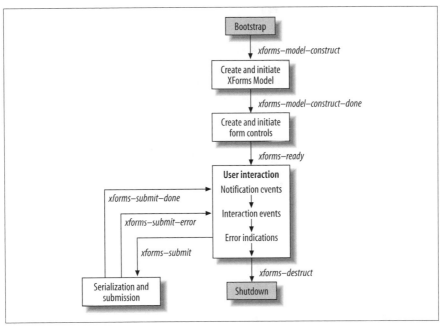

Figure 7-3. Stages of XForms processing

Initialization

> Obviously, the first step is to initialize all the machinery underlying XForms. In true committee style, the initialization process was extensively discussed, the main decision point being how much stuff gets initialized before versus after the event happens. To make everybody happy, no fewer than three separate initialization events were defined, some of which fire multiple times.

Interaction

> The major portion of XForms processing involves interacting with the user, to the end of producing an XML document. During interaction, two different kinds of events are important: events that provide a notification that something happened, and events that *cause* something to happen. Both kinds of events are important to form authors.

Submit

Sending the form data on its way is the goal of most forms, at least in theory. In practice, the submission attempt might not get very far, such as when the form contains invalid data. Other problems too, such as a crashed server, can prevent the submission from completing. For this reason, the submission process includes extra events that help the form author determine whether the submission was successful.

Deinitialization

In HTML forms, submitting the form and loading a new page always happened at the same time. In XForms, however, the author has more granular control of the process. Thus, even though there is a single deinitialization event, it's still worth discussion of when it happens.

Error Condition

Error processing is a tricky subject. In HTML forms, nearly any error is tolerated without generating error messages (but often at the expense of erratic or unpredictable behavior). In XForms, any number of problems can cause a fatal error, which will prevent a form from displaying properly.

Useful Events

Following the approach in Chapter 4, the following sections categorize events into the useful and (politely) less-useful categories. Most of these events come from the XForms specification, but a few truly useful ones come from other places. Events are one of four major types:

lifecycle

An event that deals with setting up or tearing down the XForms engine.

notification

An event indicating something took place.

interaction

An event that triggers some kind of processing. Cancelling the event (when that is possible) stops the default processing.

error handling

An event indicating an error or some other unusual situation occurred.

Another important part of the description of an event is whether it bubbles, and whether it is cancelable, in terms of XML Events. Each event description contains all of the preceding information.

The DOMActivate Event

Event type: (From DOM Level 2 Events) **Event target element:** form control, possibly other elements such as hyperlinks

Bubbles: Yes **Cancelable:** Yes

DOMActivate is probably the event most commonly used by XForms authors. Activation in this context can mean a mouse click, pressing the **Enter** key, or any other action indicating the user has requested that something special should happen.

Even though a DOM isn't guaranteed to be present in an XForms engine, this event will always work as described here.

The DOMFocusIn and DOMFocusOut Events

Event type: (From DOM Level 2 Events) **Event target element:** form control, possibly other elements such as hyperlinks

Bubbles: Yes **Cancelable:** No

These two events serve as notifications of receiving and losing focus, respectively. In XForms, they are mainly useful as a way of tracking and coordinating focus changes on form controls.

Even though a DOM isn't guaranteed to be present in an XForms engine, this event will always work as described here.

The xforms-ready Event

Event type: lifecycle **Event target element:** model
Bubbles: Yes **Cancelable:** No

This event is fired just after the entire XForms processor has been initialized and is ready to go. As such, it's the perfect place to perform any needed initialization as part of startup.

The xforms-model-construct-done Event

Event type: lifecycle **Event target element:** model
Bubbles: Yes **Cancelable:** No

When "lazy author" processing is used—when the XForms processor synthesizes instance data based only on form controls—the XForms Model is not yet initialized when this event fires. In practice, this is not a serious problem, since "lazy author" forms are typically very simplistic, and don't use XML Events or XForms Actions at all.

This initialization event occurs after the XForms Model has been initialized, but before the user interface has, making it the perfect place to perform any data-level initialization tasks, before any data shows up in a form control.

The xforms-model-destruct Event

Event type: lifecycle   **Event target element:** model
Bubbles: No   **Cancelable:** No

This event is fired as part of the shutdown sequence for the XForms engine. If any of the form logic has allocated temporary resources, this is the place to free them.

The xforms-help and xforms-hint Events

Event type: interaction   **Event target element:** form control
Bubbles: Yes   **Cancelable:** Yes

These events indicate that a help or hint message is about to be displayed to the user. It can be useful to perform other processing at this time. It can also be useful in some cases to cancel the event, which will prevent the help or hint from rendering. Finally, it can also be useful to dispatch this event to a form control to provide help or hint on demand.

The xforms-reset Event

Event type: interaction   **Event target element:** model
Bubbles: Yes   **Cancelable:** Yes

This event indicates that the form is about to be reset. In some situations, it might be necessary to prevent a reset from happening, in which case the event can be terminated, blocking the reset. Otherwise, a listener for this event is a good chance to do any last-minute processing before everything in the XForms Model resets to its initial state.

The xforms-submit Event

Event type: submission   **Event target element:** submission
Bubbles: Yes   **Cancelable:** Yes

This event indicates that the form is about to be submitted. In some situations, it might be necessary to prevent submission from happening, in which case the event can be terminated, blocking the submission. Otherwise, a listener for this event is a good chance to do any last-minute processing before the form data gets packaged and sent over the wire.

The xforms-value-changed Event

Event type: notification   **Event target element:** form control
Bubbles: Yes   **Cancelable:** No

This event serves as a notification that the value that a form control is displaying is due for a change. This normally happens at the point where the user navigates away from a changed control, since only then is it known that the user has finalized her choice. In this respect, xforms-value-changed is much like the onchange event from HTML.

It's also possible, however, for a form control to send additional xforms-value-changed events while the user is still interactively typing, clicking, dragging, or speaking to produce a value. In order for these extra events to be generated, the attribute incremental on the form control needs to have the value true.*

The xforms-select and xforms-deselect Events

Event type: notification   **Event target element:** item or case
Bubbles: Yes   **Cancelable:** No

These events indicate that a particular list item has been selected or deselected. Additionally, within switch elements, individual case elements will be the target of these events as they become selected and deselected.

The xforms-valid and xforms-invalid Events

Event type: notification   **Event target element:** form control
Bubbles: Yes   **Cancelable:** No

These events serve as notifications as to whether a form control is valid or invalid, and can be useful when custom error messages or validity feedback are needed. Either of these events will be dispatched only when the validity state of the form control changes.

The xforms-readonly and xforms-readwrite Events

Event type: notification   **Event target element:** form control
Bubbles: Yes   **Cancelable:** No

These events serve as notifications as to whether a form control is read-only or read-write. In most forms, every form control will be fixed as either read-only or not. The dynamic nature of the readonly model item property, however, means that the writability of a form control can change pretty much at any time. Either of these events will be dispatched only when the read-only state of the form control changes.

---

* For the select and select1 form controls, incremental="true" is the default, so the extra events will normally be dispatched as the selection interactively changes.

The xforms-required and xforms-optional Events

Event type: notification
Bubbles: Yes
Event target element: form control
Cancelable: No

These events serve as notifications as to whether a form control is required or optional. In most forms, every form control will be fixed as either required or not. The dynamic nature of the required model item property, however, means that the requirement of a form control can change pretty much at any time. Either of these events will be dispatched only when the required state of the form control changes.

The xforms-enabled and xforms-disabled Events

Event type: notification
Bubbles: Yes
Event target element: form control
Cancelable: No

These events serve as notifications as to whether a form control is enabled or disabled, as controlled by the relevant model item property. Normally, a form is designed so that different form controls become relevant on an as-needed basis, which makes this notification especially common and useful. Either of these events will be dispatched only when the relevant state of the form control changes.

The xforms-out-of-range and xforms-in-range Events

Event type: notification
Bubbles: Yes
Event target element: form control
Cancelable: No

These events serve as notifications that a form control isn't able to display the current value for some reason. For example, a range control might only be capable of controlling values between 0 and 100, and yet be bound to a value of 150 in the instance data. select1 controls are also limited to displaying values defined in item or itemset elements, and thus can become out of range when initial values are applied. Either of these events will be dispatched only when the relevant state of the form control changes.

The xforms-submit-done Event

Event type: notification
Bubbles: Yes
Event target element: submission
Cancelable: No

This event is a notification that a form submission has successfully completed. In HTML forms there was no way to tell when (or if) the submission was done, so this event is a welcome addition for form authors.

Less-Useful Events

The following XForms events are included here for completeness, even though they are not very useful for form authors.

The xforms-rebuild, xforms-recalculate, xforms-revalidate, and xforms-refresh Events

Event type: interaction   **Event target element:** model
Bubbles: Yes   **Cancelable:** Yes

These events essentially serve bookkeeping purposes for the XForms engine, and receive little use for form authors. xforms-rebuild causes the data structures used for recalculation to be reinitialized, xforms-recalculate performs the actual calculation, xforms-revalidate checks the validity of instance data nodes, and xforms-refresh causes the form controls to reflect the latest condition of the XForms Model. Several notification events provide a better way to keep track of the status of individual form controls: xforms-valid and xforms-invalid, xforms-readonly and xforms-readwrite, xforms-required and xforms-optional, and xforms-enabled & xforms-disabled.

DOM Mouse Events

Event type: (From DOM Level 2 Events)   **Event target element:** most elements
Bubbles: Yes   **Cancelable:** Yes (except mousemove)

Mouse events, especially click, should be avoided whenever possible. These events can't be reliably used in XForms, since there's no guarantee that a DOM will be present, or that the device rendering XForms will even have a mouse. Instead, device-independent events, such as DOMActivate, should be used.

DOM Keyboard Events

Event type: (From DOM Level 3 Events)   **Event target element:** varies
Bubbles: Yes   **Cancelable:** Yes

DOM Level 2 Events avoided the area of keyboard events. A Working Draft of Level 3 does include key events, but the future of that specification is uncertain. These events can't be reliably used in XForms, however, since there's no guarantee that a DOM will be present, or that the device rendering XForms will even have a keyboard. In general, it is better to use an abstract event, such as DOMActivate, instead of hardware-specific keyboard events.

DOM Mutation Events

Event type: (From DOM Level 2 Events) **Event target element:** any element
Bubbles: Yes **Cancelable:** No

DOM Mutation Events serve as notifications to various changes in the DOM structure. These events can't be reliably used in XForms, however, since there's no guarantee that a DOM will be present. Instead, more general events such as xforms-value-changed should be used.

The xforms-model-construct Event

Event type: lifecycle **Event target element:** model
Bubbles: No **Cancelable:** No

This is the first XForms-related event a document will see; it provides the initial hook into XForms Processing. While this event is propagating, nothing is initialized, not even instance data. As such, this event is more useful to XForms implementers than authors.

The xforms-focus Event

Event type: interaction **Event target element:** form control
Bubbles: No **Cancelable:** Yes

This event causes focus to change to the target form control. Unless you have a specific reason for not using the XForms Action setfocus, this event is generally not needed by form authors. For notifications of focus changing, DOMFocusIn and DOMFocusOut are the best way to keep tabs on focus.

The xforms-insert and xforms-delete Events

Event type: notification **Event target element:** instance
Bubbles: Yes **Cancelable:** Yes

These events initiate the processing needed to add or remove nodes from repeating sets, and serve primarily as bookkeeping events for XForms.

The xforms-next and xforms-previous Events

Event type: interaction **Event target element:** form control
Bubbles: No **Cancelable:** Yes

These events indicate the user's intention to navigate forward or backward, relative to the overall navigation order of the form, such as when the Tab key is pressed (though other ways to accomplish navigation are possible, depending on the device in question). There are few useful things that XForms authors can do with these events. DOMFocusIn and DOMFocusOut generally serve as better notifications to keep track of focus.

The xforms-scroll-first and xforms-scroll-last Events

Event type: notification

Event target element: repeat or other element with repeat attributes

Bubbles: Yes

Cancelable: No

Originally, these events were intended to allow repeating items to be dynamically loaded from a database, on demand as the user scrolled through the list. This turned out to be more difficult than it looked. As a result, these events have little use for XForms authors.

Error Handling

Inevitably, problems can happen during form processing. XForms defines events for such situations, with each event categorized as either an *error*, which is recoverable, or an *exception*,[*] which is serious enough to immediately terminate form processing with a message.

When an error condition occurs, application-specific handling (such as logging) is always a possibility and, in fact, is a good way to investigate problems.

The xforms-submit-error Event

Event type: error handling

Event target element: model

Bubbles: Yes

Cancelable: No

This event indicates that the submit process failed to successfully complete.

The xforms-binding-exception Event

Event type: error handling

Event target element: any element that can hold a binding expression

Bubbles: Yes

Cancelable: No

This event indicates that some critical problem was found in a binding expression, such as an XPath syntax error, an improperly connected reference from an IDREF to an ID, or duplicated bind elements.

---

[*] Those with some programming background might think of an exception as something that can be "caught," in order to prevent a terminating error condition. XForms 1.0, however, doesn't provide any means to catch or re-throw an exception, so they're always fatal.

The xforms-link-exception Event

Event type: error handling   **Event target element:** model
Bubbles: Yes   **Cancelable:** No

This event indicates that an unrecoverable error occurred when attempting to refer to some external resource. This can happen when an external initial instance fails to load from the src attribute in the instance element.

The xforms-link-error Event

Event type: error handling   **Event target element:** model
Bubbles: Yes   **Cancelable:** No

This event indicates that a particular remote resource had a problem, but that processing will continue. Some elements, such as label, can refer to a remote resource and also a local resource as a fallback. When the remote resource fails to load, the local resource will be used instead.

The xforms-compute-exception Event

Event type: error handling   **Event target element:** model
Bubbles: Yes   **Cancelable:** No

This event indicates that an unrecoverable error occurred during processing of computes. This can be caused by an XPath syntax error, a circular dependency, or bad parameters to certain XPath functions.

CHAPTER 8

Submit

"This element encodes how, where, and what to submit."
—XForms Candidate Recommendation,
12 November 2002, section 3.3.3,
"The submission Element"

Data collection is a multibillion-dollar industry, so it's not surprising that XForms includes a rich set of options for submitting form data. Getting data out of old HTML forms is an exercise in jumping through hoops, due largely to the limited data format defined for forms—name/value pairs generally. XForms can still provide data in these legacy formats, though it shines the brightest when sending XML data.

The four main questions in submitting form data are *when*, *what*, *where*, and *how*. The following sections discuss each of these questions.

When to Submit

Submit happens when the user presses the big button labeled "Submit," right? Well, sure, but there's more to the story than that.

Formally, a submission is initiated when an event called `xforms-submit` arrives at the `submission` element (described in detail later in this chapter) For more on XML events, see Chapter 7. The reason for a separate event is so that submission can be requested in other situations, such as pressing Enter or meeting other conditions. The XForms Action `send` can explicitly send out the submission event, and the form control named `submit`, which otherwise behaves exactly like `trigger`, also dispatches an `xforms-submit` event, thus providing the click-to-submit feature...except that dispatching the `xforms-submit` event doesn't guarantee that the submission will complete successfully. Several things have to happen first:

- The event has to actually reach its target element. The previous chapter discusses event processing, which includes ways to stop an event before it reaches its mark. If the event gets blocked for any reason, no submission happens.

- Another submission on the same XForms Model must not be in progress already. Countless Internet surfers have suffered from duplicated message postings, or duplicated orders (or worse) because of clicking on a (seemingly) unresponsive submit button more than once. Clicking submit multiple times is safer under XForms processing because all clicks after the first will be ignored, at least until the submission completes and the user has been notified.

- The form data must validate. One of the first things that submit processing does is to perform a full validation of the instance data in question. If any problems are found, the XForms processor will send out notifications to the invalid form controls and stop the submit-in-progress. This additional processing is a major benefit of XForms over earlier web forms systems.

- Finally, it's possible for problems, such as a crashed server that can't accept any data, to occur during the submit process. In such cases, the submission can't be successful, and a notification event is sent.

Once a submit is underway, one of two things will always happen: either an `xforms-submit-done` event will be dispatched to the originating `submission` element, or an `xforms-submit-error` event will be dispatched to the `model` element that contains the originating `submission` element.

What to Submit

XML comes in trees, but sometimes trees need to be pruned. For situations where less than the full tree of instance data is needed for submission, XForms defines ways to reduce the amount of XML that gets selected for submission.

One of the most powerful techniques for managing complexity is to divide and conquer using multiple XForms Models. For example, if a web page has one form for a search tool and another to register for a newsletter, these should be in separate `model` elements. When arranged that way, each XForms Model will have separate instance data to be submitted.

Another common case is when temporary data, such as a lookup table, is needed during form processing but not during submission. Using multiple `models` can help here, too, but the strong separation between XForms Models can get in the way. Another option is to use multiple `instances`, which can use either inline or remote XML, within the same model. A special XPath function, instance( ), provides easy access to other instances (XPath data models, to be specific), as long as they are part of the same XForms Model.

In this example, the primary instance data, which the author intends for submission, is given the identifier submitme. The secondary instance data, loaded from a separate XML document and given the identifier taxrate, contains a single element such as <tax>0.725</tax>, containing a decimal tax rate. By replacing this file at any time, a new tax rate can be used in the form, thus helping separate business rules from the rest of the form.

```
<xforms:model>
  <xforms:instance id="submitme">
    <my:item>
      <my:listprice>14.00</my:listprice>
      <my:tax/>
    </my:item>
  </xforms:instance>
  <xforms:bind nodeset="/my:item/my:tax" calculate="../my:listprice *
instance('taxrate')"/>
  <xforms:instance id="taxrate" src="taxrate.xml"/>
</xforms:model>
```

In this example, the calculate expression multiplies two values. One is ../my:listprice, which refers to an element node, from which a numeric value is taken. The other is instance('taxrate'), which returns the top-level element node from the instance data associated with the ID taxrate. The result is placed in the element node at /my:item/my:tax.

Once a particular instance document is selected, XForms still provides additional ways to prune the XML tree. One way is to specify a subtree of the instance data that gets submitted, using either the ref attribute (XPath expression) or bind attribute (IDREF to a bind element).

Finally, any node that has a relevant property that evaluates to false will not be present in the submitted data. A moment of thought will show that once a node is lopped off the tree in this way, all descendent nodes (attributes, text, child elements, etc.) will also be gone, regardless of their individual relevant property

Sometimes, an author might want something to be non-relevant for UI purposes, but not want the data excluded from the XML. In the following example, the spouse element is only relevant when the user has a spouse; but since the submitted XML needs to be DTD-valid, the spouse element needs to be submitted, even if empty.

Example 8-1. Submit processing of relevant nodes

```
<xforms:model>
  <xforms:instance>
    <my:personinfo>
      <my:name>Enter your name here</my:name>
      <my:hasspouse>0</my:hasspouse>
      <my:spouse>Enter spouse's name here</my:spouse>
    </my:personinfo>
  </xforms:instance>
  <xforms:bind nodeset="/my:personinfo/my:spouse"
relevant="instance('submitpending') or ../my:hasspouse"/>
  <xforms:submission action="http://submit.example.com" method="get">
    <xforms:setvalue ref="instance('submitpending')">1</xforms:setvalue>
  </xforms:submission>
  <xforms:instance id="submitpending">
    <flag>0</flag>
  </xforms:instance>
</xforms:model>
...
```

In Example 8-1, during normal processing, the only part of the relevant expression that matters is ../my:hasspouse. This causes a form control bound to my:hasspouse to get rendered only when the user has indicated that he or she actually has a spouse. During submit processing, however, the setvalue action sets the flag in the secondary instance data to 1, causing the earlier relevant expression to always be true. As a result, the spouse element will not be excluded from the submitted XML. Note that in a real-world form, a listener for xforms-submit-error events targeted to the model should be included, to set the flag back to 0 after an unsuccessful submission attempt.

Where and How to Submit

The questions of *where* and *how* are closely related, because the target of submission is a URI. The first part of a URI, called the *scheme*, indicates the general approach for the submit transaction, as in "http," "file," or "mailto." The remainder of the URI gives more specific information on where the destination for the data is to be.

Additionally, there need to be rules for how the in-memory instance data gets written down as a pattern of bytes on the wire. In addition to XML, several backward-compatible formats included in XForms are described in the following sections.

URI Scheme and Method

URI schemes, included as part of the action attribute on submission, are the broadest selector of where and how form data gets submitted. A more fine-grained distinction is the *request method* (often just simply called "method"), which defines details about the relationship between a URI and the representation of whatever resides at that URI.

The most common request method is GET, which is used for requesting most web pages, images, sound, and video through a web browser. GET is commonly used with forms, too, especially shorter ones. The second most common method is POST, which is described in the definition of HTTP/1.1 at RFC 2616 as the preferred way to provide:

- Annotation of existing resources
- Posting a message to a bulletin board, newsgroup, mailing list, or similar group of articles
- Providing a block of data, such as the result of submitting a form, to a data-handling process
- Extending a database through an append operation

In any case, the actual function performed by the POST method is determined by the server and is usually dependent on the URI that is part of the operation.

A third request method is PUT—little used on the Web today, but hopefully something that XForms can help change. A PUT is also a write operation but, unlike POST, it implies that an existing resource indicated by the URI is getting replaced, rather than annotated or appended to. If there is no preexisting resource, then the PUT method has the effect of creating a new resource.

In XForms terms, the attribute method on submission indicates the author's selection of request method. The combination of URI scheme and method defines the overall processing that will happen during submit. Note, however, that nonsensical combinations are possible—such as "mailto:" with PUT or "file:" with POST.

http or https

The http scheme is the staple of the Web. The https scheme is functionally equivalent, except that contents in transit are encrypted so that prying eyes can't read the contents on the wire.

When to Use GET

The advent of web services has caused a considerable amount of discussion on the question of when to use GET rather than POST in HTTP. SOAP 1.1 defined only a POST binding which, when combined with a proliferation of point-and-click tools, led to an initial surge in the popularity of POST (and a corresponding decline in the popularity of GET).

A back-to-basics movement called REST (Representational State Transfer, formalized in the PhD thesis of Apache developer Roy T. Fielding), however, has shifted emphasis back to the virtues of GET. The W3C SOAP 1.2 effort, for example, has added machinery to allow SOAP calls to take place through a simple HTTP GET.

The W3C Technical Architecture Group (TAG) has also weighed in, issuing "URIs, Addressability, and the use of HTTP GET" at *http://www.w3.org/ 2001/tag/doc/get7*. As far as this relates to form authoring, a good rule of thumb is to always first consider using GET, which will produce a bookmark-able result—in other words, creating an "addressable" resource that anyone on the Web can access just by entering a URL in their browser. The exception, when POST is preferable, occurs when one or more of the following is true:

- The form has a large amount of data, which will usually be the case when an upload form control is present.
- Submitting the form causes some significant obligation, such as placing an online order.
- Form data is sensitive enough that it shouldn't be included in the URI, as it appears in the browser location bar or server logs, which will usually be the case when a secret form control is present.

One possible option to avoid the entire GET versus POST controversy is to use PUT instead. This method is best suited for situations where a form is tied to a single resource, so that the form can be considered a specialized editing or document creation tool for XML.

GET, POST, and PUT all make sense for form data sent via the http scheme, under the right conditions. All conforming XForms processors are guaranteed to support http. The https scheme, however, might not be present on certain small devices that don't support the necessary encryption routines.

file

The file scheme represents access to the local filesystem. On the Windows platform, networked file shares, which are treated in a similar fashion to the local file system, can also be accessed through the file URI scheme.

Only PUT makes sense for form data sent via the file scheme. Since not every XForms processor is guaranteed to have a filesystem, this scheme isn't guaranteed to be supported.

The file scheme can be useful when used indirectly with relative paths. For example, the following declaration

```
<submission method="put" action="myfile.xml"/>
```

specifies that the action URI is relative. When the containing document is loaded from a file scheme, then the submission also goes to the file myfile. xml in the current directory. When the containing document is loaded from an http scheme, however, the submission gets PUT to a URI in the same directory as the current document, except ending in myfile.xml.

On DOS and Windows file systems, absolute file paths contain a drive letter. The official Internet standards are silent on how to include drive letters, especially since the colon character is reserved for a different purpose. As a result, there is no universally agreed-upon way to describe a file URI with a drive letter. Some variations in use include:

```
file:/C:/dir/file.xml
file://C:/dir/file.xml
file:///C:/dir/file.xml
file:///C|/dir/file.xml
file:///C%3A/dir/file.xml
```

UNC paths, starting with a double backslash, have a similar set of ambiguities when mapped to the file URI scheme.

mailto

The mailto scheme represents an electronic mailbox, to which messages may be posted.

Only POST makes sense for form data via the mailto scheme. Since not every XForms processor includes mail functionality, this scheme isn't guaranteed to be supported.

Others...

Any other URI schemes not listed here should be used only if you are in a controlled environment (such as an intranet) where you can ensure that browsers will support it, or if the form is non-critical and of little consequence to users who find that submit doesn't work.

Support for additional URI schemes is considered an extension to XForms, which is covered further in Chapter 11.

Serialization Formats for Data Submission

At some point the in-memory instance data gets converted, or *serialized*, into a stream of bytes suitable for sending over the wire. The following sections describe the serialization formats defined in XForms 1.0.

application/xml

XML for form data submission is one of the main motivations behind XForms. This is the most straightforward serialization format; after all, instance data is based on the XPath data model, which was specifically designed to model XML.

XForms borrows from XSLT several attributes that fine-tune the serialization process: indent, encoding, omit-xml-declaration, standalone, and cdata-section-elements. Note that these attributes maintain the original spelling, including dashes, as in XSLT. The following section describing the submission element contains all the details on what each attribute does. The important thing to note is that all of these attributes taken from XSLT are advisory only, and that an XForms processor is free to ignore any that are inconvenient for the implementer.

The media type of the submitted XML will be application/xml by default, though this can be overridden with the mediatype attribute.

Another attribute, includenamespaceprefixes, is the part of XForms that has to do with details of how namespaces are generally handled in XML-based specifications. The XPath data model contains, for each element node, one namespace node per in-scope namespace. As a result, inline instance data will have additional, generally unwanted, namespace nodes that get serialized. Example 8-2 shows code that will give this result.

Example 8-2. Serialization of namespace nodes

```
<xforms:instance>
  <my:data/>
</xforms:instance>
```

In Example 8-2, the XForms namespace is in scope, bound to the prefix xforms. Correspondingly, the XPath data model will contain a namespace node for the XForms namespace and, without taking any special action, the serialized XML will look like this:

```
<my:data xmlns:xforms="http://www.w3.org/2002/xforms"/>
```

In other words, the end result includes an unnecessary namespace declaration. Because of the widespread use of namespace prefixes in attribute values and text, it's not always safe to throw away unused prefixes. The solution is to specify the includenamespacesprefixes attribute, which will cause any prefixes that are not visibly used (for element or attribute names) to be suppressed, unless they are included in a space-separated list. A special value, #default, applies to the default namespace. So, to prevent the unwanted xforms namespace declaration seen earlier, a simple:

```
includenamespacesprefixes=""
```

on the submission element would do the trick.

application/x-www-form-urlencoded

The algorithm for *urlencoding* is quite simple, but nevertheless has caused many problems in the past. The reason for this is that the algorithm specification, as defined in HTML, didn't say what to do with characters outside the range of ASCII. As a result, numerous variations sprang into existence, with no way to tell which was which.

XForms fixes this by mandating UTF-8 as the one true basis for urlencoding. In UTF-8, a single character is represented by a single byte for characters in the ASCII range, and by between two and five bytes for other Unicode characters. Overall, the urlencoding algorithm for a given string boils down to:

1. Replace all space characters with +, and all reserved characters with %NN, where NN represents the uppercase hexadecimal notation for the character. (Reserved characters are semicolon, slash, question mark, colon, at sign, ampersand, equals, plus, dollar sign, and comma.)

2. Replace all characters outside of ASCII range with the (multiple byte) representation of that character in UTF-8, with each byte in turn represented as %NN, as above.

For example, the string "Ünited Stätes" after urlencoding, would be "%C3%9Cnited+St%C3%A4tes".*

---

* According to *The Onion*, 29 April 1997, the U.S. Congress planned to toughen the image of the country by adding umlauts to the name.

A bigger hurdle is representing structured XML as a flat list of name/value pairs. In this, XForms doesn't attempt to model an entire tree as a flat structure. Instead, only the leaf element nodes—those that contain one and only one text child node—are included in the serialization. That's right—no attributes, no namespace information, and no elements that aren't leaf nodes. When such XML features are needed, application/xml is the appropriate serialization format.

The overall serialization follows the document order of the instance data, and is formatted as:

```
{element local name}={value of text node}{separator}
```

Where the element local name and value of the text node are urlencoded, separated by a literal equals character. Between each grouping is a separator character, a semicolon by default. For compatibility with older systems, this character can be changed to an ampersand through the separator attribute on submission (the ampersand is no longer favored, because it needs to be specially escaped as & when represented in XML).

multipart/related

One drawback of application/xml, and especially of urlencoded data, is that binary content can't be represented efficiently. The answer to this dilemma is a media type that allows binary content to be packaged separately from XML. A number of MIME types that start with multipart/, though originating as part of the global email system, have come into use as a way to package binary data along with XML.

All of the multipart formats break a message into smaller pieces, simply called parts. In multipart/related, the first part contains XML serialized just as in the application/xml serialization method. Subsequent parts contain binary resources that the user selected through <upload> form controls, which must be bound to instance data nodes of the XML Schema datatype anyURI.

For example, a simple form might capture an employee name as a string and a photo as an anyURI, like this:

```
<xforms:input ref="name">
  <xforms:label>Name</xforms:label>
</xforms:input>
<xforms:upload ref="picture" mediatype="image/*">
  <xforms:label>Photo</xforms:label>
</xforms:upload>
```

Serialized as `multipart/related`, the result would be:

```
Content-Type: multipart/related; boundary=a42113842b; type=application/xml;
start"=<000000@dubinko.info>"
Content-Length: 65232
--f93dcbA3
Content-Type: application/xml; charset=UTF-8
Content-ID: <000000@dubinko.info>
<?xml version="1.0"?>
<root_element>
  <name>Cordova Cassanova</name>
  <picture>cid:000001@edubinko.info</picture>
</root_element>
--a42113842b
Content-Type: image/jpg
Content-Transfer-Encoding: binary
Content-ID: <000001@dubinko.info>
...binary image data...
--a42113842b--
```

Notice that the URI of the picture has been dereferenced, and the actual data now appears in the submitted data stream.

 If the instance data contains encoded binary data, through the XML Schema `base64Binary` or `hexBinary` datatypes, for example, `multipart/related` is a poor choice of a serialization format, since the encoded binary data will appear inline in the first XML part, not as separate parts.

multipart/form-data

This serialization format, which is already widely deployed across the Web due to the `<input type="file">` control in HTML forms, doesn't take any special advantage of XML. Following the same rules as `application/x-www-form-urlencoded`, every leaf node is treated as a separate part, each of which can exist in a separate encoding. Since individual sections can include binary characters without the overhead of escape characters, the overall data size can be much smaller than other serialization formats.

The technique this serialization format uses can lead to a proliferation of parts in a multipart stream, which can lead to overhead for larger bodies of instance data. For content that would otherwise be base64Encoded or hexEncoded, however, it can provide a substantial savings.

What Happens After Submit?

If you've ever bought something online, after submitting the order, you've probably seen a page that says "please print this for your records." One of the capabilities of HTTP is that a GET or POST returns a result page.

When looking at the response to a submission, there are two main things to consider: Does the response contain a body? And was the submission attempt successful? If the attempt is non-successful, then the form will always remain in the current display (or auditory context, or whatever). If the submission is successful, however, more results are possible.

In HTML forms, the response from a form submission always replaces the entire currently displayed document. This behavior is also the default in XForms, and is expressed through the attribute replace="all" on <submission>. Other possible values for that attribute open other interesting possibilities. One possibility is replace="instance", which takes an XML-based response and replaces the just-submitted instance data with the newly-arrived stuff. Another option is replace="none", which disregards any response document. Future versions of XForms might offer even more possibilities, such as replacing only part of the instance data.

For any replacement to happen, the response must include a body. In many cases (such as mailto or file submission), there won't be any response body.

The submission Element

submission

The submission element defines the parameters for serializing and submitting instance data. An XForms Model can contain any number of submission elements. The content model for this element is any XForms Action element, which is convenient when dealing with events that target this element.

Most of the action takes place in the attributes of this element.

ref *and* bind

> These attributes are functionally equivalent to binding attributes (see Chapter 5), and are used to select a particular node that is selected, along with all its children. (Note that the model attribute is unnecessary, since the enclosing XForms Model is always the one under consideration.) If neither of these attributes are present, all of the instance data, as defined by the first <instance> element, is selected for submission.

action *(required)*

This attribute holds a URI to which the submission will be directed.

method

This required attribute provides additional information that, combined with the URI scheme in the action attribute, determines how the submission process will proceed. Possible values are "get", "put", "post", "form-data-post", "urlencoded-post", or any QName that includes a prefix. QName values are considered extensions, as discussed in Chapter 11.

replace

This attribute describes what should happen with the response document (if any) that is returned from the submission action. Possible values are "all", "instance", "none", or any QName that includes a prefix. QName values are considered extensions, as discussed in Chapter 11. The default value is "all".

separator

This attribute, which applies only to urlencoded serialization, specifies the separator character to be used between name/value pairs. Possible values are "&" or ";". The default is ";".

includenamespaceprefixes

This attribute, which applies only to application/xml serialization, contains a space-separated list of namespace prefixes, possibly including the special value of "#default", which represents the default namespace. Namespace prefixes that appear in the list are ensured to be present in the serialized XML instance data. When this attribute is not present, no special processing happens, and thus instance data that originates inline will generally have extra namespace declarations. Possible values are boolean values, as defined by XML Schema datatypes.

version *(from XSLT)*

This attribute, which applies only to application/xml serialization, advises the XML serializer to insert a particular version number in the XML declaration, such as:

```
<?xml version="1.0"?>
```

indent *(from XSLT)*

This attribute, which applies only to application/xml serialization, advises the XML serializer to insert whitespace, with the intent of producing visually formatted XML. Possible values are boolean values, as defined by XML Schema datatypes.

encoding *(from XSLT)*

This attribute, which applies only to application/xml serialization, specifies the preferred character encoding that the XML serializer should use to encode sequences of characters as sequences of bytes, such as:

```
<?xml version="1.0" encoding="ISO-8859-1"?>
```

`omit-xml-declaration` *(from XSLT)*

> This attribute, which applies only to `application/xml` serialization, advises the XML serializer to not include an XML declaration. Possible values are boolean values, as defined by XML Schema datatypes.

`standalone` *(from XSLT)*

> This attribute, which applies only to `application/xml` serialization, advises the XML serializer whether it should include a standalone declaration, such as:
>
> ```
> <?xml version="1.0" standalone="yes"?>
> ```
>
> Possible values are boolean values, as defined by XML Schema datatypes.

`cdata-section-elements` *(from XSLT)*

> This attribute, which applies only to `application/xml` serialization, contains a space-separated list of element names that the XML serializer is advised to output the text content of as CDATA sections.

mediatype

> This attribute selects the Internet media type to be associated with the serialized instance data, and has a default of `application/xml`.

Review: Submission Options

As a general rule, the URI scheme and serialization method can be chosen as follows.

Your first instinct should be to use GET with `application/x-www-form-urlencoded`, unless your solution meets one of the good reasons not to use GET, mentioned earlier in the "When to Use Get" sidebar. For everything else, consider first using POST with `application/xml`, unless you need to be compatible with a "legacy" server that's expecting submissions from clients running HTML forms or similar applications. Table 8-1 summarizes.

Table 8-1. Guidelines for XForms submit

When you have this scenario...	...use a submission element such as this
Your solution produces a small amount of data, which contains no sensitive information and doesn't trigger any significant obligations.	`<submission method="get" action="`*http URI*`"/>`
Your solution has to work with a server configured to accept GET requests from HTML forms.	`<submission method="get" separator="&amp;" action="`*http or https URI*`"/>`
Your solution creates new XML data.	`<submission method="put" inlcudenamespaceprefixes="" action="`*http, https, ftp, or file URI*`"/>`

Table 8-1. Guidelines for XForms submit (continued)

When you have this scenario...	...use a submission element such as this

Your solution feeds XML data into a larger processing system.	`<submission method="post"`
	`includenamespaceprefixes=""`
	`action="http, https, or mailto URI"/>`

Your solution has to work with a server configured to accept standard POST requests from HTML forms.	`<submission method="urlencoded-post"` `action="http or https URI"/>`
Your solution has to work with a server configured to accept file uploads from HTML forms.	`<submission method="form-data-post"` `action="http or https URI"/>`
Your solution produces XML data that includes lots of embedded binary data.	`<submission method="form-data-post"` `action="http, https, or mailto URI"/>`
Your solution includes `<upload>` controls that accept anyURI data.	`<submission method="multipart-port"` `action="http, https, or mailto URI"/>`

Security and Privacy Concerns

Form data can contain sensitive information. What's more, it can be initialized with a `file` URI scheme, which has the capability of pulling data from the hard drive of anyone who loads a form. Combine this with an XML Events-powered submit that occurs as a part of form loading, and you have the potential for a serious privacy breech. Using the `file` scheme, a hostile XForms document could also potentially overwrite files on the hard drive of the person viewing the document.

Browser vendors over the years have gradually learned their lessons and incorporated restrictions in their products to prevent these kinds of abuses. Still, an important part of authoring an XForms solution is to stop and think about what could go wrong, and testing is a key part of that process.

CHAPTER 9
Styling XForms

"Never offend people with style when you can offend them with substance."

—Sam Brown

A key advantage of XForms over proprietary forms systems is that content and presentation are separated. The presentation aspect fits in well with other W3C technologies, namely Cascading Style Sheets (CSS), a technology that predates even XML. As of this writing, CSS is undergoing two concurrent revisions, one labeled Level 2.1, a general clean-up of an earlier specification, as well as Level 3, which includes more advanced features. This chapter discusses aspects of CSS that XForms brings to the fore. If you are not already familiar with the fundamentals of CSS, I suggest picking up the book that taught me most of what I know about CSS, Eric Meyer's *Cascading Style Sheets: The Definitive Guide* (O'Reilly).

CSS, Level 3

The XForms specification includes an example of XForms-specific CSS code in an appendix. Example 9-1 reproduces this sample:

Example 9-1. Sample CSS from the XForms specification

```
@namespace xforms url(http://www.w3.org/2002/xforms/);
/* Display a red background on all invalid form controls */
*:invalid { background-color: red; }

/* Display a red asterisk after all required form controls */
*:required::after { content: "*"; color: red; }

/* Do not render non-relevant form controls */
*:disabled { visibility: hidden; }
```

Example 9-1. Sample CSS from the XForms specification (continued)

```
/* The following declarations cause form controls and their labels
to align neatly, as if a two-column table were used */
xforms|group { display: table; }
xforms|input { display: table-row; }
xforms|input > xforms|label { display: table-cell; }
xforms|input::value { border: thin black solid; display: table-cell; }

/* Display an alert message when appropriate */
*:valid   > xforms|alert { display: none; }
*:invalid > xforms|alert { display: inline; }

/* Display repeat-items with a dashed border */
*::repeat-item { border: dashed; }

/* Display a teal highlight behind the current repeat item */
*::repeat-index { background-color: teal; }

/* Display non-relevant repeat items in the system GrayText color */
*::repeat-item:disabled { visibility: visible; color: GrayText; }
```

The CSS selectors mentioned in the XForms appendix are listed in Table 9-1.

Table 9-1. CSS selectors mentioned by XForms

Selector	Type	Description
:required	pseudo-class	Selects any form control considered required by the rules of XForms.
:optional	pseudo-class	Selects any form control not considered required by the rules of XForms.
:valid	pseudo-class	Selects any form control considered valid by the rules of XForms.
:invalid	pseudo-class	Selects any form control considered invalid by the rules of XForms.
:read-only	pseudo-class	Selects any form control considered read-only by the rules of XForms; most other elements are normally read-only as well.
:read-write	pseudo-class	Selects any form control considered writable by the rules of XForms.
:out-of-range	pseudo-class	Selects any form control considered out-of-range by the rules of XForms.
:in-range	pseudo-class	Selects any form control considered in-range by the rules of XForms.

Table 9-1. CSS selectors mentioned by XForms (continued)

Selector	Type	Description
::value	pseudo-element	Represents the data-entry area of a form control, excluding the label
::repeat-item	pseudo-element	Represents a single item from a repeating sequence, as discussed in Chapter 6.
::repeat-index	pseudo-element	Represents the current item of a repeating sequence, as discussed in Chapter 6.

A specification called *CSS3 Basic User Interface Module* officially defines these selectors, and a number of additional useful properties. (The information in this chapter is based on the Last Call Working Draft version of that specification. See *http://www.w3.org/TR/css3-ui/* for updates.).

CSS Box Model

While this chapter does not provide a complete reference to CSS, readers might find it helpful to review a few of the less familiar concepts. One key concept to keep in mind throughout these sections is the CSS *box model*. As you recall, the box model provides a nested series of rectangular regions, such as margins, borders, and padding, each of which can be individually styled. Figure 9-1 shows how this works.

For things such as form controls, normally each element is styled in its own box model, which forces the styling to fit within the constraints of the document structure. There are two notable exceptions. A pseudo-class is a way of applying CSS to something not directly present in the markup structure of a document, like the first line of text in a paragraph or a form control that is currently "valid." A pseudo-element is similar, though it is possible to locate specific points where a *fictional tag sequence* of implied start and end tags are affected by the style rules. These fictional tags are not visible through 'View Source, the DOM, or any other means. They only serve to help specify how CSS properties inherit to different parts of an XML document.

The Appearance Property

CSS Level 3 defines a new property named appearance. Even though the aforementioned XForms appendix doesn't use this property, form authors find it to be one of the most useful CSS properties. It allows, for example, a select1 element to be rendered specifically as radio buttons, or a pull-down menu, or any of a large number of options. The property has a broad-rang-

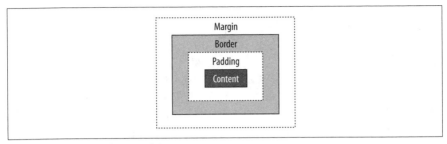

Figure 9-1. The CSS box model

ing effect on the rendering of an element, and can change color, font, background, padding, border, margin, and other properties. It's important to note, however, that this CSS property affects only the rendering of the element. For example, applying an appearance value of pull-down-menu to any given element won't make it suddenly start behaving as a data collection tool. To be useful, the element has to have a predefined set of data collection semantics, as XForms nicely provides, leaving CSS just to control the details of presentation.

Other than a few special values ('normal' and 'inherit'), the predefined values for this property are:

- icon
- window
  - document
  - workspace
  - desktop
  - tooltip
  - dialog
- button
  - push-button
  - hyperlink
  - radio-button
  - checkbox
- menu
  - menubar
  - pull-down-menu
  - pop-up-menu
  - list-menu
  - radio-group

- checkbox-group
- outline-tree
- field

The values are arranged as five general purpose categories with more specific sub-categories. When one of the more specific properties isn't recognized, it is to be treated as the more general one.

The application of CSS properties is, strictly speaking, distinct from the appearance attribute on form control elements. Using attribute value selectors, however, it is possible to take control of exactly how a form control is rendered for various values of the appearance attribute. The following CSS code in Example 9-2 demonstrates:

Example 9-2. Using the appearance attribute to fine-tune how form controls render

```
select1[appearance="minimal"] { appearance: pop-up-menu; }
select1[appearance="compact"] { appearance: list-menu; }
select1[appearance="full"]    { appearance: radio-group; }
```

> The selectors in Example 9-2 show a more convenient syntax with regard to XML namespaces. In CSS Level 3, if no default namespace is declared (through an @namespace rule), the selectors will match all elements named select1, no matter what namespace the elements are in. Additionally, each rule contains an attribute selector in square brackets that further refines the selection.

The first selector shown selects all select1 elements that have an attribute appearance="minimal", applying the declaration {appearance:pop-up-menu;}. The second and third rules perform a similar function.

Aligning Form Controls and Labels

Consider this section of CSS code:

Example 9-3. CSS to align form controls and labels

```
@namespace xforms url(http://www.w3.org/2002/xforms/);

/* The following declarations cause form controls and their labels
to align neatly, as if a two-column table were used */
xforms|group { display: table; }
xforms|input { display: table-row; }
xforms|input> xforms|label { display: table-cell; }
xforms|input::value { border: thin black solid; display: table-cell; }
```

The above set of rules uses the namespace-aware rules of CSS Level 3 to provide special layout rules for `input` elements appearing in a group. The `display: table` rule, in combination with `display: table-row` and `display: table-cell`, cause the same layout effect as if HTML tables had been used.

Note, however, that even with actual tables, this kind of layout wouldn't be possible, because of the way the CSS box model interacts with form controls. Each form control has a child `label` element, which can be styled using the techniques described in this chapter. Additionally, each form control has a wrapper element bearing the name of the form control, such as `input`, `select`, or `range`. Any styling applied to this wrapper affects the overall form control, and any styles not specifically overridden will inherit to the label, too. Thus, a style rule such as:

```
input { background-color: blue; }
```

will color the background of both the label and the actual data entry area a lovely shade of electric blue.

A common request is to style just the data entry area, typically with a border or background color, without affecting the label. The difficulty is that no element exists that directly represents the data entry region of a form control. This is a good example of a case where CSS pseudo-elements are needed, as shown in Figure 9-2. In CSS terminology this can be described by a *fictional tag sequence*, which shows pseudo-elements along with the normal elements, even though the pseudo-elements aren't visible through View Source, the DOM, or any other means. Figure 9-2 illustrates how CSS rules can address the different parts of form controls.

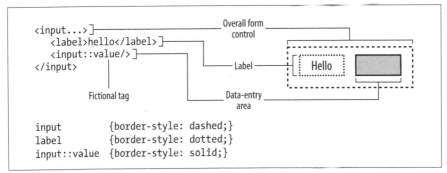

Figure 9-2. Styling a form control with a pseudo-element

Taking advantage of the pseudo-element, the style rules at the beginning of this section cause a group element to be treated as a table, an `input` element as a table-row, and the `label` element and the data entry area pseudo-element as table cells. Note that the table layout algorithm defined by CSS properly accounts for languages with a right-to-left reading order, so that in such cases, the label will appear on the right-hand side, as expected.

 Despite being part of CSS Level 2 since 1998, CSS table layout is still poorly supported. It remains to be seen whether XForms will spark better implementations of this feature.

As a result of these rules, form controls can be presented in a nicely aligned grid, as shown in Figure 9-3, which is based on the code shown in Example 9-4:

Example 9-4. Aligned form controls and labels

```
<group>
  <input bind="email">
    <label>E-Mail Address</label>
  <input>
  <input bind="rank">
    <label>Rank</label>
  </input>
  <input bind="serial">
      <label>Serial Number</label>
  </input>
</group>
```

E-Mail Address	
Rank	
Serial Number	

Figure 9-3. Form control alignment

Styling Invalid Form Controls

Consider this CSS rule in Example 9-5:

Example 9-5. Style rule for invalid form controls

```
/* Display a red background on all invalid form controls */
*:invalid { background-color: red; }
```

The above rule selects form controls based on the :invalid pseudo-class, giving all invalid controls a red background. Note that due to the dynamic nature of CSS, the form controls will change appearance as soon as the XForms processor is able to make the determination of validity. As a result, form controls will have an overall red background, as shown in Figure 9-4.

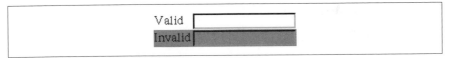

Figure 9-4. Invalid form control

Of course, if the goal is to have just the data entry portion of the form control change color, then the style rule needs to select only the ::value pseudo-element, as shown in Example 9-6:

Example 9-6. Improved style rule for invalid form controls

```
/* Display a red background on all invalid form controls */
*::value:invalid { background-color: red; }
```

Figure 9-5 shows how this might look.

Figure 9-5. Invalid form control, with pseudo-element styling

Styling Required Form Controls

Consider this CSS rule in Example 9-7:

Example 9-7. Style rule for required form controls

```
/* Display a red asterisk after all required form controls */
*:required::after { content: "*"; color: red; }
```

The above rule selects form controls based on the :required pseudo-class, producing generated content (an asterisk) for elements that match the rule. As a result, any form controls that are required for submission will have an asterisk appear just after in the rendered content, colored red by an additional rule, as shown in Figure 9-6.

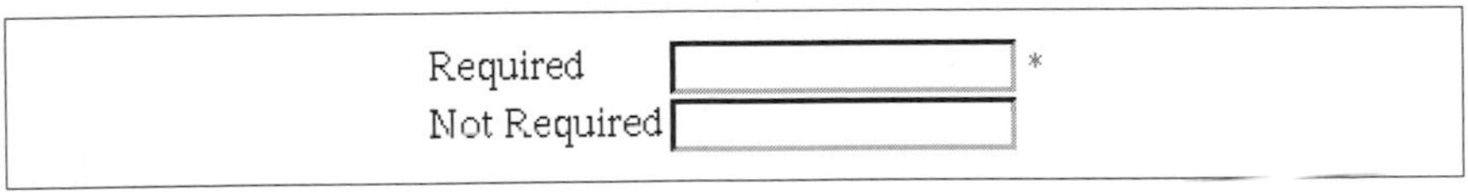

| Required | | * |
| Not Required | | |

Figure 9-6. Required form control

Styling Alert Messages

Consider these two CSS rules in Example 9-8:

Example 9-8. Style rules to selectively display an error message

```
/* Display an alert message when appropriate */
*:valid   > xforms|alert { display: none; }
*:invalid > xforms|alert { display: inline; }
```

These rules alter the visibility of the alert element, selected as part of the XForms namespace, based on the validity of the form control. When valid, the element is set to display:none, which removes the content from the document flow altogether. Otherwise, the content is set to display: inline, which causes the text to appear in the document, as shown in Figure 9-7.

Valid	xyzzy@plugh.info
Invalid	xyzzy Invalid email address

Figure 9-7. Alert messages

Styling Repeating Items

Consider these two CSS rules in Example 9-9:

Example 9-9. Style rules for repeating items

```
/* Display repeat-items with a dashed border */
*::repeat-item { border: dashed; }

/* Display a teal highlight behind the current repeat item */
*::repeat-index { background-color: teal; }
```

Repeating items also present a unique situation for styling, since the original document tree contains only a single repetition. Thus, XForms defines a pseudo-element for each repetition, which allows style rules to be associated with each repeat item. Also, since repeating groups have a special concept of a current index, an additional pseudo-element allows the current repeat index to be styled as well, as shown in Figure 9-8.

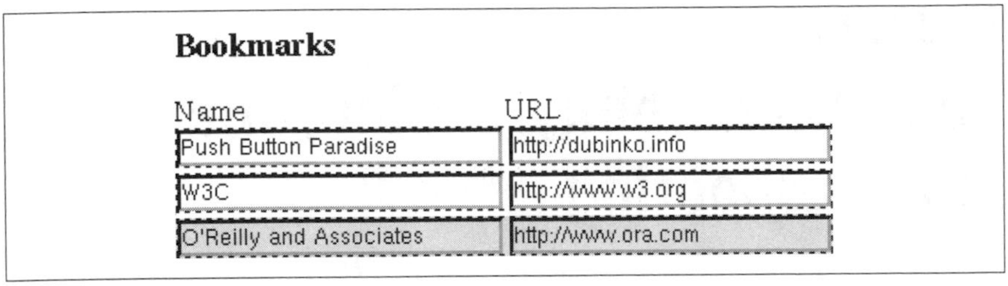

Figure 9-8. Repeating items, with one active

Styling Non-Visible Items

Finally, consider this CSS rule in Example 9-10:

Example 9-10. Style rule for the current repeat item

```
/* Display non-relevant repeat items in the system GrayText color */
*::repeat-item:disabled { visibility: visible; color: GrayText; }
```

The final example from the XForms appendix shows one way of controlling the appearance of non-relevant form controls, which use the existing CSS properties :enabled and :disabled. The code above shows how, when individual members of a repeat group are invalid, they can be rendered in a different color. In this case, it is the special GrayText color, which varies depending on local operating system settings, but it is typically a lower-contrast rendition of the normal system text. Figure 9-9 shows one possible rendering for invalid text, which appears on the second line.

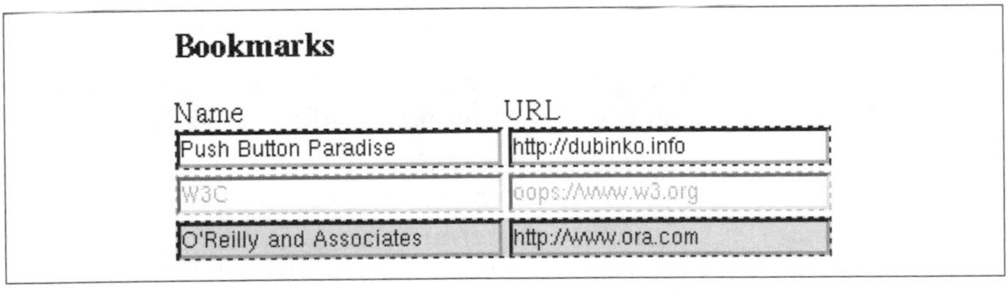

Figure 9-9. Controlling display of non-relevant form controls

CHAPTER 10

Form Accessibility, Design, and Troubleshooting

*"There are two ways of constructing a software design:
One way is to make it so simple that there are obviously
no deficiencies, and the other way is to make it so
complicated that there are no obvious deficiencies."*
—C. A. R. Hoare

The next time you visit your favorite web site, try reading the page using only the view source command in your web browser. Can you make sense of the information there, or do you have to pick through a forest of extraneous tags inserted by the site's designers for visual layout? Browsing page source is a rough approximation of how many users experience web pages when using a screen reader, assistive technology that helps compensate for physical limitations such as blindness. The practice and study of creating web content that doesn't shut out such readers is called *accessibility*.

Accessibility matters, even for forms and web pages that don't have an expected audience of users with special visual or other needs. For example, even sighted persons are interested in eyes-free browsers, and making content accessible is closely related to improving usability. Designing an accessible web interface is often simply a matter of awareness of the many ways in which people use the Web (see *http://www.w3.org/WAI/EO/Drafts/PWD-Use-Web/*). Many devices are beginning to support speech interfaces, either alone or in combination with conventional visual interfaces. Other devices simply have limited processing capabilities, due to size or other constraints. No matter what the reason, keeping in mind principles of good design and accessibility is just good sense.

Later, this chapter covers some common design patterns for forms, some XForms-specific tips and tricks, and some guidelines for transitional issues.

Basics of Accessibility

When producing web content, the most important thing you can do to help accessibility is to directly say what you mean. Prefer an image over a multimedia plug-in application. Prefer ordinary text over an image with text in it. Don't use a table unless you are providing truly tabular information. When the structure of your document and the structure of the markup align, current and future assistive technologies (not to mention users!) will have an easier time making sense of your information.

The view-source test is one of the simplest tests of accessibility, and it doesn't require any additional hardware or software. It shouldn't take an accessibility expert to create accessible web pages. To help developers in this regard, the World Wide Web Consortium (W3C) has released a series of documents providing guidelines for developers on how to create accessible web pages.

W3C Accessibility Guidelines

Version 1.0 of the W3C Web Content Accessibility Guidelines became a Recommendation in May 1999. A Version 2.0 with updated and simplified guidelines is currently proceeding through the W3C Recommendation track. Associated with each guideline are one or more specific techniques, found in a linked document.

Version 1.0 of the Web Content Accessibility Guidelines at *http://www.w3.org/TR/WCAG10/* contains the following fourteen suggestions:

1. Provide equivalent alternatives to auditory and visual content.
2. Don't rely on color alone.
3. Use markup and style sheets and do so properly.
4. Clarify natural language usage.
5. Create tables that transform gracefully.
6. Ensure that pages featuring new technologies transform gracefully.
7. Ensure user control of time-sensitive content changes.
8. Ensure direct accessibility of embedded user interfaces.
9. Design for device-independence.
10. Use interim solutions.
11. Use W3C technologies and guidelines.
12. Provide context and orientation information.
13. Provide clear navigation mechanisms.
14. Ensure that documents are clear and simple.

Each guideline is divided into a number of checkpoints, each of which has a priority of one, two, or three, with one being the most important. Conformance to the guidelines is then based on multiple levels, with "A" meeting all priority 1 guidelines, "Double-A" meeting all priority 1 and 2, and "Triple-A" meeting all priority 1, 2, and 3. Note that the conformance levels themselves are spelled out so that text-to-speech systems will correctly render the phrase.

Of these checkpoints, the following fall into the category of basic good design, not specifically applicable to XForms: 1, 2, 3, 4 (through use of xml: lang attributes), 5, 7, 10, 12, and 14. The following come almost automatically by using XForms: 8, 9, and 11. Using a new technology like XForms actually makes it harder to fulfill point 6, since screen readers usually lag behind even mainstream browsers in adoption of new technologies. During a transitional period, it might be necessary for accessible pages that use XForms to maintain a fallback to a page that uses the older XHTML forms. The remaining point, number 13, can be accomplished for form controls through the careful use of host-language techniques for controlling navigation order and keyboard access, discussed in the "XForms-specific Design Hints" section.

Form Design Patterns

A design pattern is a recurring set of solutions to common problems, written down in such a way as to help designers apply them to new problems—avoiding the pain of having to rediscover them. The popular 1995 book *Design Patterns: Elements of Reusable Object-Oriented Software* (Addison-Wesley)[*] helped make many developers aware of design patterns. Since then, many other fields, mostly computer-related, have agreed upon design patterns. The following sections describe design patterns for XForms, including the four pieces of information that *Design Patterns* made popular. Each pattern includes:

1. A problem definition
2. A solution description
3. A discussion of consequences and trade-offs

Each section also contains sample code to illustrate the pattern.

[*] By the so-called "gang of four": Gamma, Helm, Johnson, and Vlissides.

Stepwise XPath

Problem: XPath expressions used by XForms can get extremely complicated, and keeping track of context nodes and other details can obscure the details of what's happening in a form.

Solution: It is possible to author a form in such a way that the only XPath expressions used are simple names, much like the departing HTML forms technology. To do this, the structure of the user interface elements must match the structure of the instance data. Additional levels of UI nesting can be accomplished with group elements, so that instance data like this:

```
<purchaseOrder>
  <items>
    <item partNum="1234">
      <quantity/>
    </item>
  </items>
</purchaseOrder>
```

would have a matching user interface like this:

```
<group name="items">
  <group name="item">
    <input ref="@partNum">...</input>
    <input ref="quantity">...</input>
  </group>
</group>
```

Note that the root element purchaseOrder, already a default context node, doesn't need a supporting group element.

Consequences: This design pattern is mutually exclusive with the Design by Buddy System pattern, which doesn't use XPath binding expressions on form controls. The resulting XPath expressions contain no complicated syntax, and (other than the leading @ symbol for attributes) could pass for the simple names used in HTML forms. One disadvantage is that extra syntax is needed, to provide nested group elements that each provide a single step in the XML path. A hybrid approach could use a single outer group element, with a full XPath expression, like this:

```
<group name="items/item">
  <input ref="@partNum">...</input>
  <input ref="quantity">...</input>
</group>
```

Design by Buddy System

Problem: Designing a form takes both technical skills, to get the data portions operating correctly, and graphical design skills, to make the layout attractive and easy to use. Often, a single person doesn't have all the necessary skills.

Solution: XForms makes it possible to divide form authoring cleanly between two individuals or teams. One person can design the XML and data side, and the other can lay out the form controls. The key to dividing the labor is in the interface between form controls, which can use the bind attribute to provide a consistent and XPath-free interface. Using this system, the designers would first come up with a list of the needed form controls, assigning each one a short name, something like that shown in Table 10-1.

Table 10-1. Form design by buddy system

Description	Type	Name
User's first name	Data entry	fname
User's last name	Data entry	lname
Web preference	Choice of 'flash', 'java', or 'html'	webpref
User's password	Password entry	pass

From this agreement, the data designer could begin authoring the XForms Model, including the structure of the XML to be submitted, and any validations or calculations needed. As part of authoring, a number of bind elements will need to be created. For each, the data designer assigns the id from the Name column above. The result, using a mythical xml:id attribute, would look something like this:

```
<xforms:model>
  <xforms:instance>
    <session>
      <name>
        <given/>
        <family/>
      </name>
      <pref/>
      <password/>
    </session>
  <xforms:instance>
  <xforms:submission ... />
  <xforms:bind nodeset="name/given" xml:id="fname" ... />
  <xforms:bind nodeset="name/family" xml:id="lname" ... />
  <xforms:bind nodeset="pref" xml:id="webpref" ... />
  <xforms:bind nodeset="password" xml:id="pass" ... />
</xforms:model>
```

At the same time, the graphical designer can begin incorporating XForms form controls into the layout of the web or printed page. For each form control, the graphic designer applies a bind attribute with a name agreed upon earlier, producing something like this:

```
...
  <xforms:input bind="fname" ... />
...
  <xforms:input bind="lname" ... />
...
  <xforms:select1 bind="webpref" ... />
...
  <xforms:password bind="pass" ... />
...
```

The result is a fully-functional form; to those filling out the form, there would be no apparent differences between this and a single-source authored form.

Consequences: This design pattern is mutually exclusive with the Stepwise XPath pattern. Overall, designing a form in this manner is slightly more work overall, though that is offset by dividing the work into two parts.

XML Localization

Problem: Different users often prefer different languages, and in current form systems it is very difficult to deliver a form that is in the desired language. Conventional form engines usually have to dynamically assemble a form every time it's delivered, so it's not much additional effort to dynamically place all the text on the form. In XForms, however, it's more common to have a static form, with dynamic XML data.

Solution: Pervasive throughout XForms is the idea that any content presented to the user should be able to have roots in XML instance data. This is true for form controls, labels, help/hint/alert messages, and XForms Actions such as message and load. Even ancillary text can be taken from XML and displayed using the output form control. For example, a form like this:

```
<p>Please complete the following questions:</p>
<input bind="term">
  <label>Search:</label>
</input>
<select bind="where">
  <label>Search the following areas of the web site:</label>
  <item>
    <label>Product Information</label>
    <value>p</value>
  </item>
  <item>
```

```
      <label>Technical Support</label>
      <value>t</value>
    </item>
    <item>
      <label>Developer Resources</label>
      <value>d</value>
    </item>
  </select>
```

might be changed so that all displayed strings come from a secondary instance document:

```
<p><output ref="instance('strings')/msg.top"/></p>
<input bind="term">
  <label ref="instance('strings')/label.term"/>
</input>
<select bind="where">
  <label ref="instance('strings')/label.where"/>
  <item>
    <label ref="instance('strings')/label.where.item1"/>
    <value>p</value>
  </item>
  <item>
    <label ref="instance('strings')/label.where.item2"/>
    <value>t</value>
  </item>
  <item>
      <label ref="instance('strings')/label.where.item3"/>
    <value>d</value>
  </item>
</select>
```

Note that no strings intended for presentation to the user remain. Each place where a string used to be is replaced by a reference to an instance named strings, with an informal naming convention. The addition of one line to the XForms Model:

```
<instance id="strings" src="path-to-xml-file.xml"/>
```

points to an external XML file containing the strings. The file would look something like this:

```
<strings>
  <msg.top>Please complete the following questions:</msg.top>
  <label.term>Search:</label.term>
  <label.where>Search the following areas of the web site:</label.where>
  <label.where.item1>Product Information</label.where.item1>
  <label.where.item2>Technical Support</label.where.item2>
  <label.where.item3>Developer Resources</label.where.item3>
</strings>
```

With all the strings in a single place, it could easily be translated into something else, say, Spanish.

```
<strings>
  <msg.top>Favor de terminar las preguntas siguientes:</msg.top>
  <label.term>Buscar:</label.term>
  <label.where>Busque las áreas siguientes del Web site:</label.where>
  <label.where.item1>Información de Producto</label.where.item1>
  <label.where.item2>Ayuda Técnica</label.where.item2>
  <label.where.item3>Recursos para Desarrolladores</label.where.item3>
</strings>
```

Modern web servers have the capability to perform content negotiation, delivering a file in a language requested by a particular browser. Using this capability, a single static form can be delivered in multiple languages. For example, instructions for Apache can be found at *http://www.apacheweek.com/features/negotiation*.

Consequences: Overall, this technique involves significantly more setup than just hard-coding a single language. Setting up a web server to deliver different versions of a file based on language preferences can still be difficult, though the situation is improving. On the other hand, compared to the effort of re-creating the same form over and over again in different languages, this technique is more efficient when many languages need to be supported.

XForms-specific Design Hints

The following sections describe various small tips and tricks—too small individually to be considered a design pattern—for authoring XForms content.

Always Include Keyboard Navigation Hints

Every XForms document should include enough information to provide a well-though-out navigation sequence, encompassing both form controls and other elements, such as hyperlinks, from the host language. The exact details on how to do this will vary depending on the host language, though XForms provides a sample implementation based on an attribute called navindex.

Form controls that will be frequently accessed should also include a keyboard shorcut; the details of which are again provided by the host language. The following code shows one possible way to accomplish this, in a host language that uses the techniques suggested by XForms.

```
<input ref="passwd" accesskey="P" navindex="3">
  <label>Password:</label>
</input>
```

Always Use P3P Datatypes

The least understood model item property in XForms is probably p3ptype. The W3C P3P specification defines a comprehensive set of rules about identifying what kinds of data collection take place on a web site, at a very granular level. P3P includes rules to define such datatypes, but of main interest to XForms authors are the built-in types defined as part of the base data schema.

Adding the p3ptype property during form authoring is easy, and it provides one huge benefit: autofill. Most browsers have adapted to allow the values in forms to be recalled and repopulated later, removing the need to have to re-enter information. This works by looking at the name and label of the form control. In XForms, labels can include markup, or even refer to instance data or other files. And instead of simple names, form controls have an XPath expression. Combined, these aspects make it harder for an XForms browser to tell reliably whether two controls from different forms are really collecting the same data.

P3P datatypes neatly solve this problem. As a model item property, p3ptype associates to the actual data, not to the form control, which is a view on the data. Some examples:

```
<bind nodeset="first_name" p3ptype="user.name.given"/>
<bind nodeset="last_name" p3ptype="user.name.family"/>
<bind nodeset="screen_name" p3ptype="user.login.id"/>
<bind nodeset="password" p3ptype="user.login.password"/>
<bind nodeset="year_of_birth" p3ptype="user.bdate.ymd.year"/>
<bind nodeset="home_telephone" p3ptype="user.home-info.telecom.telephone"/>
<bind nodeset="company_name" p3ptype="business.name"/>
<bind nodeset="spouse_name" p3ptype="thirdparty.name.given"/>
```

For more details and examples, refer to the P3P specification at *http://www.w3.org/TR/P3P/*.

Don't Use a Form for Navigation

As of this writing, it is still common for web sites to use forms (usually a drop-list) for navigation purposes. You select something from the list, and you're whisked away to another page. This approach is increasingly unnecessary as XHTML 2.0 advances, such as including a special element nl for navigation lists. In SVG or other languages, it might, at times, still be necessary to use forms for navigation, but the most specific tool available is usually the right one to use. If you have no choice but to use XForms for navigation, code along the following lines will do the trick.

```
<select1 ref="..." appearance="minimal">
    <item>
        <label>Go to destination 1</label>  <value>...</value>
        <load ev:event="xforms-select"
        resource="http://url-for-destination-1" show="replace"/>
    </item>
    <item>
        <label>Go to destination 2</label>  <value>...</value>
        <load ev:event="xforms-select"
        resource="http://url-for-destination-2" show="replace"/>
    </item>
</select1>
```

Concatenating a Currency Symbol or Special Character

Some commonly requested features are possible in XForms, though not obviously so. One such task is concatenating a currency symbol to an entered value. As an example, if the user enters "100", the value that ends up in the data should really be "€100". The catch is that if the user gets clever and initially enters "€100", it should still work.

This can be accomplished using the if( ) function:

```
<bind nodeset="cost" calculate="if( starts-with(€, '?'), ., concat( '?',€
))"/>
```

This calculation gets a little confusing with all the dots, which represent the current value. Another way to think of it is as pseudo-code:

```
if ( current value starts with currency symbol )
   return current value
else
   return currency symbol concatenated with current value
```

Instead of hard-coding a currency symbol, the appended string could easily be taken from elsewhere in the instance data. Accomplishing this is left as an exercise for the reader.

Server-Side Database Lookups

A popular feature in advanced form systems is the ability to perform a lookup based on a remote database. For example, a governmental system might want to call up taxpayer details based on a unique identifier. Privacy issues alone, not to mention sheer size, prevent this from working in the local context. So, what's needed is a way to submit a partially valid form to a server, to get a partial response back.

In XForms, this is possible through the `replace` attribute on the element `submission`. A form submission always results in a response. Normally, the response is a new web page to display in place of the form that was just submitted. It is possible, however, to get an XML response back that is used as new instance data for the form—exactly what is needed for database look-ups.

One complication is that the form at the time of initiating the·lookup might be only partially completed. Normally, this would cause problems on any data items that are considered required. The workaround is to include a special flag that temporarily relaxes required validations, like this:

```
<model>
  <instance id="main">...</instance>
  <bind nodeset="some_data" required="instance('strict_flag')"/>
  <submission id="send_data" ... />
  <submission id="do_lookup" replace="instance" ... />
  <instance id="strict_flag">
    <flag>true</flag>
  </instance>
</model>
```

With code such as this in place, a `trigger` kicks off the database lookup:

```
<trigger>
  <label>Lookup</label>
  <action ev:event="DOMActivate">
    <setvalue ref="instance('strict_flag')">false</setvalue>
    <send submission="do_lookup"/>
  </action>
</trigger>
```

The sequence of XForms Actions used here first sets the strict flag to false, then submits the data. By referencing the `submission` element with an ID of `do_lookup`, the response from the server (which must be XML-suitable as instance data) is used to continue with the form.

Database validations can be achieved in a similar manner, by returning a validity flag in the XML.

Reliably Submitting the Form with Enter

Popular search engines pride themselves on a minimal interface—typically just a single entry box with a search button. In most cases, the button isn't even necessary. Just hitting enter in the entry box is enough. This useful functionality, however, has never been standardized before. In fact, one search engine detects that you've pushed the button instead of just hitting enter and responds with a tip, as shown in Figure 10-1.

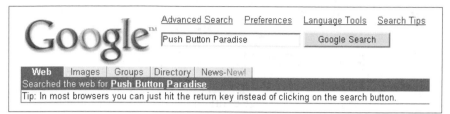

Figure 10-1. The unreliable effects of the Enter key

Tip: For most browsers you can just press the Return or Enter key, instead of clicking on the search button.

In XForms, this can be accomplished reliably. Even better, the solution isn't dependent on the Enter key, so it will work on cell phones, voice browsers, and other such systems.

The answer lies with the DOMActivate event, which occurs for a form control when the Enter key (or some equivalent) is, pressed or activated. XML Events take care of the rest, given code like this:

```
<input ref="q">
  <label>Search</label>
  <send submission="id_of_submission_element" ev:event="DOMActivate"/>
</input>
```

Refresh-on-Demand

One consideration for extremely small devices is that even refreshing the display can take long enough that it would be annoying if it happened automatically. In such situations, it is possible to disable all automatic refreshing, instead using a trigger to explicitly refresh on demand.

Through XML Events, it is possible to cancel all xforms-refresh events before they reach their target, which will prevent all automatic refreshes from happening. All that is needed is one extra attribute from XML Events, like this:

```
<model ev:event="DOMActivate" ev:propagate="stop">
  ...
</model>
```

With that change, all that is needed is a trigger to refresh manually:

```
<trigger>
  <label>Refresh Display</label>
  <refresh ev:event="DOMActivate"/>
</trigger>
```

Troubleshooting

Stubborn Read-only Controls

If all your form controls appear mysteriously read-only (or even completely missing, depending on style sheet configuration), check the namespace of instance to make sure it's not in the XForms namespace. For example, the following code looks innocent enough, but has an error.

```
<model xmlns="http://www.w3.org/2002/xforms">
  <instance>
    <purchaseOrder>
      <item/>
    </purchaseOrder>
  </instance>
</model>
```

The problem is subtle: the purchaseOrder element is appearing in the default (here XForms) namespace, which can't be right, since XForms doesn't define a purchaseOrder element. When declared this way, none of the binding expressions actually point into the instance data because of the difference in names. The result: all form controls behave as if they were read-only.

The correct thing to do is to put the purchaseOrder in the proper namespace with an xmlns declaration. Even if the instance data is not in a namespace, then the special declaration xmlns="" must be used to undeclare the default namespace, like this:

```
<model xmlns="http://www.w3.org/2002/xforms">
  <instance>
    <purchaseOrder xmlns="">
      <item/>
    </purchaseOrder>
  </instance>
</model>
```

Of course, if the instance data is in a specific namespace, then the code above would need to contain the namespace URI instead of an empty string.

Context Node Problems

Another problem that can cause individual form controls or groups of form controls to misbehave is forgetting what the XPath context node is in a given situation. The default rules for context nodes make the common cases the most straightforward, though more advanced work remains tricky. An incorrect assumption about what the context node is will typically cause an XPath expression to select an empty node-set, which is an invalid binding for a form control.

The basic rule is that the context node starts out at the top-level element node. If instance data resembles this:

```
<top-level>
  <child>
    <grandchild>
  </child>
</top-level>
```

then the proper way to bind to grandchild as the default instance is either of the following, using relative and absolute paths respectively:

```
bind="child/grandchild"
bind="/top-level/child/grandchild"
```

The same goes for references using this instance( ) function. The default context node is the top-level element node. Thus, the way to bind to grandchild in a non-default instance is the following:

```
bind="instance('elsewhere')/child/grandchild"
```

Note that references to non-default instances don't have a direct analogue to an absolute path.

XForms Portion of Document Not Recognized

Another common situation can cause XForms readers to malfunction: most HTML (and even XHTML) documents are served with a media type of text/ html, which is never appropriate for a document containing XForms. One workaround is to define a new file extension, .xhtml, for all XHTML documents, then configure the web server to deliver those files with a proper media type of application/xhtml+xml. On some web servers, this can be done by adding to (or creating, if necessary) a file named *.htaccess* in the root directory for documents, containing this line:

```
AddType application/xhtml+xml;charset=utf-8;qs=0.999 .xhtml
```

Schema or Validation Errors

In XForms 1.0, it is almost always an error to bind a form control to an element node that can have other element children. This mistake is easy to make in some XML vocabularies. For example, in UBL, the XML structure for containing line item part numbers is:

```
<cat:OrderLine>
  <cat:Item>
    <cat:SellersItemIdentification>
      <cat:ID>Enter part number here</cat:ID>
```

It is easy to mistakenly think that the element named SellersItemIdentification is a container for part number data when, in fact, the child element ID is. Thus, an erroneous UI binding expression like this:

```
<xforms:input ref="cat:OrderLine/cat:Item/cat:SellersItemIdentification" .
..>
```

will create mixed content, with text followed by the still empty ID element. This will cause either data loss, when a downstream process doesn't find the data where expected, or a more immediate Schema validation error, when text is detected in a location where it doesn't belong.

Making the Switch to XForms

From a technology perspective, XForms makes a clean break with HTML forms. The reality, though, is that, as of 2002, nearly every Web site is using HTML forms or, more precisely, is expecting visiting browsers to be equipped to handle HTML forms and JavaScript. Given the slow rate at which new technologies reach average users, it will likely be several years before Web designers can safely rely on XForms being present as a standard feature of visiting browsers. This section contains some pointers on how to make a smooth transition to XForms technology.

Client-Side and Server-Side XForms

HTML forms were defined such that the only reasonable way to implement the technology was in a client-side browser. XForms, on the other hand, defines things such as validation rules and declarative actions, which can be processed on either a client or a server. This gives a lot of flexibility in the architecture of an XForms engine and, in many cases, allows XForms to be layered on top of existing browser technologies.

One common strategy for XForms engines is to divide processing between the client and server. The dividing line between client and server can be in several different places:

The Featherweight Client

The client side requires almost no intelligence, serving only as a viewer application, while the server handles all of the logic and processing. Frequent server round trips are needed in order to coordinate the display with the internal state of the engine. The open source Chiba project (*http://chiba. sourceforge.net*) falls into this category.

The Scriptable Client

The client side includes a scripting engine or some limited ability to do local processing, which can perform some of the logic and calculations. Only the most sophisticated operations require a server round trip, improving the user experience.

The Modern Browser Client

The server "compiles" the form definition into a dense bundle of HTML, CSS, and JavaScript that existing browsers will render in a way scarcely distinguishable from a native XForms engine. If the target browser has XML capabilities, the resulting XML can be directly submitted. Otherwise, the server needs to reinterpret a conventional form submission as XML. The IBM XML Forms Package (*http://www.alphaworks.ibm.com/tech/xmlforms*) includes a server-side compiler that falls into this category.

One major benefit of XForms split architectures is that they are readily adaptable to various supported languages in the client, including HTML, SVG, and VoiceML, among other possibilities. In particular, HTML translation is a popular option for supporting XForms in existing clients.

Client-Side Options

Another way to work with XForms today is to take advantage of the plug-in architecture of modern browsers. Two of the most popular options are the DENG engine (*http://mozquito.markuplanguage.net*), which works with any Flash 6 enabled browser, and FormsPlayer (*http://www.formsplayer.com*), which turns the most popular browser, IE6 for Windows, into a full-fledged XForms engine.

CHAPTER 11

Extending XForms

"Still, what an arm! and I could alter it:
But all the play, the insight and the stretch—
Out of me, out of me!"
—Robert Browning

To wrap up this book, this chapter will delve into the ways that XForms can be extended. Conventional HTML forms, in contrast, offered hardly any methods of extensibility, other than script and some vague wording about how the object element could be used as a form control. With XForms, extensibility is a core part of the design, which will be a key asset as the focus shifts from Version 1.0 of XForms to later versions.

The Cost of Extensibility

Extensibility is usually talked about as an obviously advantageous feature—but it has a dark side, too. The easier it is to extend a system, the harder it is to make two separate implementations of that system agree on how to behave. Perhaps this is why many standards have a tendency to have extremely complicated, feature-rich formulations in Version 1.0: fear that anything not present from the beginning will never come to pass. The customary behavior in XML applications is to ignore elements and attributes that are unknown. In many cases this works great, but other times the uncertainty of whether an element will be ignored can range from annoying to catastrophic.

XForms isn't the first technology to experience this dilemma. All of XML, to some degree, faces this set of design trade-offs. Different XML-based languages have adopted different attitudes towards extensibility. For example, XHTML 1.0 defines a strict set of elements and attributes that can't be expanded upon (at least without producing something that's not exactly XHTML—a later section discusses modularization techniques that can be used to produce new XML-based languages). SVG, in contrast, relaxes a strict content model within the foreignObject element, and W3C XML Schema allows foreign attributes anywhere. The general approach taken by the XForms specification is that XForms is a building block, to be used as a component in another language, which could have anything from a highly conservative to a highly liberal view of extensions. XForms includes a few tools to help language designers achieve the desired level of support for foreign elements.

Extension and mustUnderstand

XForms defines an official conformance level, setting the bar for the level of support This conformance level which, if you think about it, affects what's allowed in documents as well. XForms Processors are required to support the mustUnderstand attribute, which takes a value of xs:boolean. When the value is true, the element bearing the attribute is marked as something that the XForms Processor must be able to process, otherwise the form isn't even worth loading.

For example, a digital signature form control isn't defined in XForms 1.0, and would thus have to be from another namespace. As is the case with extensions, it's not guaranteed to be available. So, a prudent course for a form author would be to include a mustUnderstand attribute:

```
<vendor:signature ref="/doc/signdata" xforms:mustUnderstand="true">
...
```

On the other hand, the Extension Module isn't required for even an XForms Basic Processor to recognize. The single element, extension, is included for compound document providers and compound document types. In function, it is similar to the SVG element foreignObject, serving as an indicator that new and unusual things might be happening inside.

Both of these tools may be an important factor to consider, both for extension designers and extension users.

Ways to Extend

The designers of XForms put lots of thought into ways of making the design flexible enough to be customized at all the critical points. The following sections describe areas where XForms has explicitly been designed to be extended.

With Script

It's true that XForms eliminates the need for a great deal of scripting. But not all. This is a good thing, since any system that could replace an entire scripting language (and associated libraries) would end up nearly as complicated as what it tried to replace—or worse. Instead, if a system replaces the 20% of the most commonly used functionality, it can still eliminate 80% of the need for script.

XForms doesn't include a script element to hold any script—that's a job for the host language. Typically, a script will be called as a result of XML Events processing, as described in Chapter 7.

The XML-centric design of XForms influences the way script access to data works. Since a form at all times has a well-formed bit of XML behind it, represented by an XPath data model, script authors have a natural and familiar data structure with which to manipulate the form data. Availability of DOM access isn't a given—there's no requirement for an implementation to be based on the DOM. In fact, of the existing XPath engines, they seem to be split fairly evenly between DOM-based and not. However, in implementations that support the DOM, a special function callable from a script returns a DOM document representing the form data, which can be read, manipulated, and updated. As with other DOM interfaces, these methods are available from the scripting object representing the model element in question.

The getInstanceDocument( ) method

This method returns a DOM document that represents the current state of the instance data. One distinction about the DOM interfaces is that they are considered "live," in that they present a view of the document that stays in sync with any changes from external sources. But the DOM Document returned here is, at best, only half-live. The reason for this is that the spreadsheet-like XForms rules that ensure that changes to data are correctly propagated across the instance data do *not* take into account changes that happen due to script. For that, separate methods are needed.

The rebuild( ), recalculate( ), revalidate( ), and refresh( ) methods

Generally, after changes have been made to the DOM document retrieved from getInstanceDocument( ), the rest of the system can be updated with a sequence of calls to rebuild( ), recalculate( ), revalidate( ), and refresh( ). Overall, the code tends to look something like the following JavaScript.

```
var modelElem = document.getElementById("id_of_model_element");
var instDoc = modelElem.getInstanceDocument("id_of_instance_element");
```

```
// Perform manipulations on instDoc here ...

modelElem.rebuild( );
modelElem.recalculate( );
modelElem.revalidate( );
modelElem.refresh( );
```

 Notice that for data manipulations to affect actual form data,
the script must work with the XML DOM returned by
getInstanceDocument( ), *not* the children of the instance element. In XForms 1.0, instance data lives on a different plane
of existence than the raw document's DOM. The
getInstanceDocument( ) function provides access to this alternate plane.

Each of the four methods perform a slightly different task.

rebuild

Rebuilds a new dependency graph used by the calculation system to
determine what needs to be recalculated. When the changes to the
instance data don't add or remove any nodes, this method may be
skipped.

recalculate

Performs a recalculation, much as a spreadsheet set for manual recalculation. As a result, the values of calculated nodes might change.

revalidate

Performs a revalidation, which can result in validation messages or
changes based on :valid and :invalid selectors from a style sheet.

refresh

Actually updates the displayed form values.

As can happen in the standards process, having four separate methods to
accomplish this provides a finer level of detail than nearly any form author
would ever need. To tidy up your code, you might consider defining a single
function to handle it all, like this:

```
function fullUpdate( elem, structure_changed ) {
  if (elem) {
    if (structure_changed)
      elem.rebuild( );
    elem.recalculate( );
    elem.revalidate( );
    elem.refresh( );
  }
}
```

With New Datatypes and Libraries

One major reason for choosing XML Schema datatypes for use in XForms is that new datatypes can be defined easily. In fact, in Chapter 4, an example of a new email data type is provided.

With XPath Extension Functions

Nearly all XPath implementations provide hooks for additional functions to be defined, and also include several built-in ones. Such extensions can be used with XForms as well.

 Extension functions can be recognized by one uniform trait: they always include a namespace prefix, while those defined through the official XForms specification do not.

An XPath expression will evaluate as a syntax error if it references a function that the XPath engine doesn't know about. This can cause a problem for forms that use extension functions, since the poor user could be half-way through completing the form before the error shows up.

A special attribute, `functions`, as part of the `model` element, is the place to list (by QName) any XPath functions absolutely necessary for the form to function. The XForms processor will check this list at startup and give a suitable (and immediate) error message, if necessary.

With New Form Controls

Even though XForms defines a broad range of general-purpose form controls, others might still be needed. For example, XForms 1.0 doesn't have an electronic signature form control. While it would be straightforward for a vendor to add such a form control in another namespace, any forms that used it probably wouldn't function as expected, since the new form control would be treated as an unrecognized foreign element, and summarily ignored.

The `xforms:mustUnderstand` attribute helps a little, giving foreign elements a means to signal that they really are critical, and that it would be better to not render the form at all than to ignore a particular element, as the following example shows:

```
<vendor:signature bind="sigdata" xforms:mustUnderstand="true">
  <xforms:label>Click to sign</xforms:label>
</vendor:signature>
```

Even so, any XForms Processor that doesn't understand a special element as vendor:signature is still shut out from filling such a form, which undermines the main point of having a standard in the first place. (Determining whether a given organization considers this a feature or a bug is left as an exercise for the reader.)

With XForms Actions

XForms defines a number of elements that serve to specify declarative actions, such as setfocus, setvalue, and message. Sometimes, it is more convenient to add another declarative action than to write script. In such cases, a new element can be used as an XForms Action. As with other elements, the mustUnderstand attribute can be useful to override the ignore-if-unknown behavior that would otherwise occur.

With Custom Events

It's also possible to use events other than the DOM-defined or XForms-defined ones. For example, when a certain condition happens, you might want to send an event that a listener elsewhere in the document can do something useful with.

The element dispatch can be used to send off any event, and the XML Events machinery described in Chapter 7 can observe custom events just as well as xforms-prefixed ones.

With New Serialization Formats

Control over how form data is serialized comes from the method attribute on the submission element, and to a lesser degree, the details of the URI on the action attribute. Again, the XForms specification covers a wide range of useful values, but not every possible combination. In particular, there's no support for XML Protocol, including SOAP. (This is a planned feature for the next version of XForms. Even without the benefit of standardization, some vendors are already marching ahead with SOAP submission methods.)

Examining Microsoft InfoPath

Do not go where the path may lead;
go instead where there is no path
and leave a trail.
—Ralph Waldo Emerson

For months, people wondered what Microsoft's response to XForms would be. In the fall of 2002, Microsoft announced a new product code-named "XDocs" that appeared, at least on the surface, to be quite similar in functionality to an XForms implementation. The product came to be known officially as InfoPath and, due to the sheer size and influence of Microsoft, a subject of frequent comparison with XForms and other related technologies.

 The information in this appendix is based on the Beta 2 Technical Refresh of Microsoft Office Infopath, so some details may change.

How Does It Work?

The InfoPath application, like an XForms implementation, converts user input into a new or modified XML, which can then be fed into a back-end system. A single application is used for both designing and completing a form. InfoPath is available only on the Windows platform, as part of Microsoft Office System 2003.

An InfoPath document is stored and processed as several files, which can be either compressed into a single CAB-compressed file with a file extension of `.xsn` or stored in the same directory.

manifest.xsf

This file contains a *manifest*, or listing of all other files, as well as many other details of the form, including information on toolbars and menus associated with each *view*, information on external data sources, and error messages.

This file is roughly analogous to an XForms Model, in that it contains the non-rendered basis for a form.

*.xsl

One or more XSLT files are always included, each one defining an Info-Path view, which presents an editable view of a portion of the XML data in an InfoPath form. Each XSLT accepts the XML instance as input, and produces an output format similar to HTML forms, but augmented with several InfoPath-specific features.

The XSLT portion doesn't have an equivalent in XForms, but the HTML-like format produced by the transformation is conceptually similar to the XForms User Interface.

template.xml

This file contains the actual XML data that is edited by InfoPath. When the overall InfoPath form is published to a well-known location, the XML instance can be separately transported, via email or any other supported transport. A special pair of processing instructions included in this file help maintain the connection between the form data and the rest of the form:

```
<?mso-infoPathSolution solutionVersion="1.0.0.2" href="path/manifest.
xsf" productVersion="11.0.5329" PIVersion="1.0.0.0" ?>
<?mso-application-progid="InfoPath.Document"?>
```

When Internet Explorer encounters any XML document with these processing instructions, it attempts to launch the locally installed InfoPath application, pointing it towards the indicated manifest file.

myschema.xsd

InfoPath is strongly based on XML Schema, and the application maintains a Schema for the main XML data. A graphical "Data Source" view, while not a full-fledged Schema editor, allows the designer to make changes to the Schema.

script.js

InfoPath also includes extensive scripting capabilites, in either JScript or VBScript. If an InfoPath document contains any script, it is stored by default in this file.

It's possible for the InfoPath document to contain other user-inserted documents as well, including images, XML that can be used as a data source, and even HTML files that can be displayed in a special area called the Task Pane.

Similar, Different

How comparable is InfoPath to XForms? At a high level, both seek to overcome a similar challenge: translating user interaction into XML. Upon closer examination, however, the two technologies differ in focus, target audience, and scope.

Focus
> The InfoPath application is focused on providing a superb visual environment, of similar quality to the rest of the Microsoft Office System suite, for creating and filling out forms. In contrast, the XForms specification is designed to encourage implementations not to focus exclusively on visual media, but rather to define only the intent behind various data-gathering controls. The XForms specification gives implementations wide latitude in choices relating to how a particular form control can be implemented. Additionally, while XForms is designed to be readily produced by automated tools, InfoPath appears to be put together in such a way that only hand-designed forms are easily possible.

Target Audience
> The recommended system requirements for InfoPath demand a fairly modern Intel-compatible computer: a Pentium III or greater as well as Microsoft Windows 2000 (with Service Pack 3) or greater. Further, the software is bundled only in the Enterprise version of Office System, which is only available on a subscription basis and thus only used by larger, more Microsoft-committed organizations. On the other hand, the XForms specification was designed to work on the broadest possible range of devices, from tiny phones and PDAs to beefy servers. XForms software is being made available in a variety of packages, both open source and commercial, on an assortment of platforms.

Scope
> XForms encourages development using a defined declarative XML syntax, while InfoPath, like HTML forms, continues to encourage the deployment of script. Some interesting differences are also found in the choices of form controls supported. For example, InfoPath includes ordered and unordered lists as a form control, but doesn't support the equivalent of a multiple selection or free entry select form control. This will be explored in greater depth later in this chapter

A Real-World Example

Despite the differences, comparisons between XForms and InfoPath are inevitable. Back in Chapter 2, we examined a UBL purchase order application. It is possible to recreate that application in InfoPath, and thus compare the results. Doing so is largely a hand-to-mouse experience with the InfoPath application. The result is shown in Figure A-1.

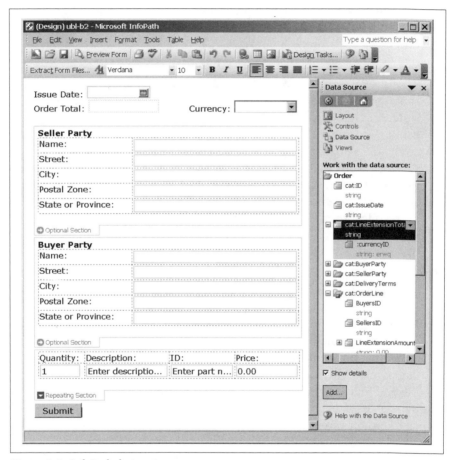

Figure A-1. InfoPath design-time

Limitations in InfoPath made a few changes necessary—for example, there is no match for the range control—but overall the solution ended up quite similar to that of XForms.

One notable difference, however, is that tables, which can be seen in Figure A-1 as dotted lines, are required for any kind of layout, which might make things more challenging for non-visual users.

The other major difference was the lack of declarative elements. In XForms, the bind element establishes a relationship that the XForms Processor sticks to at all times. In InfoPath, script attached to a number of different entry points is required. The purchase order application had four assertions to maintain:

1. A single currency code is copied into each repeating line item.
2. Since the currency code appears in two places in each line item, it is copied to the second location.
3. For each line item, the extended price is calculated as price times quantity.
4. The total of the extended price across all line items is summed up.

In XForms, these four assertions are accomplished through four bind elements:

```
<xforms:bind nodeset="cat:OrderLine/cat:LineExtensionAmount/@currencyID"
    calculate="../../cat:LineExtensionTotalAmount/@currencyID"/>
<xforms:bind nodeset="cat:OrderLine/cat:Item/cat:BasePrice/cat:PriceAmount/
@currencyID"
    calculate="../../../../cat:LineExtensionTotalAmount/@currencyID"/>
<xforms:bind nodeset="cat:OrderLine/cat:LineExtensionAmount"
    type="xs:decimal"
    calculate="../cat:Quantity * ../cat:Item/cat:BasePrice/cat:
PriceAmount"/>
<xforms:bind nodeset="cat:LineExtensionTotalAmount" type="xs:decimal"
    calculate="sum(../cat:OrderLine/cat:LineExtensionAmount)"/>
```

In InfoPath, however, the needed script is somewhat more verbose:

```
XDocument.DOM.setProperty("SelectionNamespaces",
    'xmlns:cat="urn:oasis:names:tc:ubl:CommonAggregateTypes:1.0:0.70"
    xmlns:ns1="urn:oasis:names:tc:ubl:Order:1.0:0.70"
    xmlns:my="http://schemas.microsoft.com/office/infopath/2003/myXSD/2003-
04-19T20:40:35"');

function XDocument::OnLoad(eventObj)
{
updateCurrency();
}

// This function is associated with: /ns1:Order/cat:OrderLine/cat:Quantity
function msoxd_cat_Quantity::OnAfterChange(eventObj)
{
recalcLineItem(eventObj.Site.parentNode);
recalcTotal();
}
```

```
// This function is associated with: /ns1:Order/cat:OrderLine/cat:Item/cat:
BasePrice/cat:PriceAmount
function msoxd_cat_PriceAmount::OnAfterChange(eventObj)
{
recalcLineItem(eventObj.Site.parentNode.parentNode.parentNode);
recalcTotal();
}

// This function is associated with: /ns1:Order/cat:
LineExtensionTotalAmount/@currencyID
function msoxd__LineExtensionTotalAmount_currencyID_attr::
OnAfterChange(eventObj)
{
updateCurrency();
}

function recalcLineItem( lineNode ) {
var quantity = lineNode.selectSingleNode("cat:Quantity");
var price = lineNode.selectSingleNode("cat:Item/cat:BasePrice/cat:
PriceAmount");
var extended = lineNode.selectSingleNode("cat:LineExtensionAmount");
var extPrice = parseFloat(getElementValue(quantity)) *
parseFloat(getElementValue(price));

setElementValue(extended , floatToString(extPrice, 2));
}

function recalcTotal() {
var dom = XDocument.DOM;
var extended = dom.selectSingleNode("/ns1:Order/cat:
LineExtensionTotalAmount");
var newTotal = sum("/ns1:Order/cat:OrderLine/cat:LineExtensionAmount");
setElementValue( extended, newTotal );
}

function updateCurrency() {
var dom = XDocument.DOM;
var copyFrom = dom.selectSingleNode("/ns1:Order/cat:
LineExtensionTotalAmount/@currencyID");
var lines = dom.selectNodes("/ns1:Order/cat:OrderLine");

// loop through each line item, copying in the currencyID
for (var idx=0; idx<lines.length; idx++) {
  var copyTo = lines[idx].selectSingleNode("cat:LineExtensionAmount/
@currencyID");
  copyTo.nodeValue = copyFrom.nodeValue;
  copyTo = lines[idx].selectSingleNode("cat:Item/cat:BasePrice/cat:
PriceAmount/@currencyID");
  copyTo.nodeValue = copyFrom.nodeValue;
  }
}
```

```
// Utility functions

function getElementValue( node ) {
if (node.firstChild)
  return node.firstChild.nodeValue;
else
  return "";
}

function setElementValue( node, newval ) {
if (node.firstChild) {
  node.firstChild.nodeValue = newval;
} else {
  var textnode = node.ownerDocument.createTextNode( newval );
  node.appendChild( textnode );
  }
}

function sum(xpath) {
var nodes = XDocument.DOM.selectNodes(xpath);
var total = 0;
for (var idx=0; idx<nodes.length; idx++) {
  total = total + parseFloat(getElementValue(nodes[idx]));
  }
return total;
}

function floatToString(value)
{
return "" + value;
}
```

This script approach requires a bit of care in getting and setting values from XML elements. In accordance with the DOM worldview, actual data values are stored in a text node child of the element node, except that an empty value is signified by the lack of any text child node.

On my initial attempt at this script, I neglected to attach an OnLoad entry point. The solution worked well, but had a subtle bug: if the initial value in the currency selection list was never changed, the currency value never got propagated throughout the XML. One advantage of a declarative approach is that it applies equally to initial conditions as well as the ongoing state. The XForms example didn't have to be special-cased for initialization.

Though not used here, the extensive sample forms that come with InfoPath include a large library of script that can be reused via copy-and-paste. The resulting InfoPath document can be filled out in the same application that designed the form, as shown in Figure A-2.

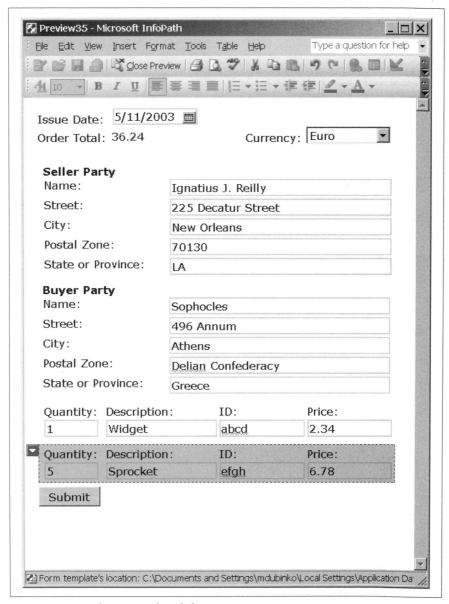

Figure A-2. Completing an InfoPath form

Conclusion

Both InfoPath and XForms are version 1.0 efforts, and both are likely to improve substantially in future revisions. For organizations that have already licensed Office System 2003, InfoPath will provide an excellent means to automate data collection tasks. For use on systems not running Office System 2003, including phones, PDAs, and PCs, XForms remains a better choice.

The GNU Free Documentation License

Published editions of this book are being released under the GNU Free Documentation License, a copy of which is provided in this appendix. The online version of this document is maintained at *http://dubinko.info/writing/xforms/*. In addition, updates, examples, and other things that didn't make it into the printed version of the book can be found there.

GNU Free Documentation License

Version 1.2, November 2002

```
Copyright (C) 2000,2001,2002 Free Software Foundation, Inc.
59 Temple Place, Suite 330, Boston, MA 02111-1307 USA
Everyone is permitted to copy and distribute verbatim copies
of this license document, but changing it is not allowed.
```

0. Preamble

The purpose of this License is to make a manual, textbook, or other functional and useful document "free" in the sense of freedom: to assure everyone the effective freedom to copy and redistribute it, with or without modifying it, either commercially or noncommercially. Secondarily, this License preserves for the author and publisher a way to get credit for their work, while not being considered responsible for modifications made by others.

This License is a kind of "copyleft", which means that derivative works of the document must themselves be free in the same sense. It complements the GNU General Public License, which is a copyleft license designed for free software.

We have designed this License in order to use it for manuals for free software, because free software needs free documentation: a free program should come with manuals providing the same freedoms that the software does. But this License is not limited to software manuals; it can be used for any textual work, regardless of subject matter or whether it is published as a printed book. We recommend this License principally for works whose purpose is instruction or reference.

1. APPLICABILITY AND DEFINITIONS

This License applies to any manual or other work, in any medium, that contains a notice placed by the copyright holder saying it can be distributed under the terms of this License. Such a notice grants a world-wide, royalty-free license, unlimited in duration, to use that work under the conditions stated herein. The "Document", below, refers to any such manual or work. Any member of the public is a licensee, and is addressed as "you". You accept the license if you copy, modify or distribute the work in a way requiring permission under copyright law.

A "Modified Version" of the Document means any work containing the Document or a portion of it, either copied verbatim, or with modifications and/or translated into another language.

A "Secondary Section" is a named appendix or a front-matter section of the Document that deals exclusively with the relationship of the publishers or authors of the Document to the Document's overall subject (or to related matters) and contains nothing that could fall directly within that overall subject. (Thus, if the Document is in part a textbook of mathematics, a Secondary Section may not explain any mathematics.) The relationship could be a matter of historical connection with the subject or with related matters, or of legal, commercial, philosophical, ethical or political position regarding them.

The "Invariant Sections" are certain Secondary Sections whose titles are designated, as being those of Invariant Sections, in the notice that says that the Document is released under this License. If a section does not fit the above definition of Secondary then it is not allowed to be designated as Invariant. The Document may contain zero Invariant Sections. If the Document does not identify any Invariant Sections then there are none.

The "Cover Texts" are certain short passages of text that are listed, as Front-Cover Texts or Back-Cover Texts, in the notice that says that the Document is released under this License. A Front-Cover Text may be at most 5 words, and a Back-Cover Text may be at most 25 words.

A "Transparent" copy of the Document means a machine-readable copy, represented in a format whose specification is available to the general public, that is suitable for revising the document straightforwardly with generic text editors or (for images composed of pixels) generic paint programs or (for drawings) some widely available drawing editor, and that is suitable for input to text formatters or for automatic translation to a variety of formats suitable for input to text formatters. A copy made in an otherwise Transparent file format whose markup, or absence of markup, has been arranged to thwart or discourage subsequent modification by readers is not Transparent. An image format is not Transparent if used for any substantial amount of text. A copy that is not "Transparent" is called "Opaque".

Examples of suitable formats for Transparent copies include plain ASCII without markup, Texinfo input format, LaTeX input format, SGML or XML using a publicly available DTD, and standard-conforming simple HTML, PostScript or PDF designed for human modification. Examples of transparent image formats include PNG, XCF and JPG. Opaque formats include proprietary formats that can be read and edited only by proprietary word processors, SGML or XML for which the DTD and/or processing tools are not generally available, and the machine-generated HTML, PostScript or PDF produced by some word processors for output purposes only.

The "Title Page" means, for a printed book, the title page itself, plus such following pages as are needed to hold, legibly, the material this License requires to appear in the title page. For works in formats which do not have any title page as such, "Title Page" means the text near the most prominent appearance of the work's title, preceding the beginning of the body of the text.

A section "Entitled XYZ" means a named subunit of the Document whose title either is precisely XYZ or contains XYZ in parentheses following text that translates XYZ in another language. (Here XYZ stands for a specific section name mentioned below, such as "Acknowledgements", "Dedications", "Endorsements", or "History".) To "Preserve the Title" of such a section when you modify the Document means that it remains a section "Entitled XYZ" according to this definition.

The Document may include Warranty Disclaimers next to the notice which states that this License applies to the Document. These Warranty Disclaimers are considered to be included by reference in this License, but only as regards disclaiming warranties: any other implication that these Warranty Disclaimers may have is void and has no effect on the meaning of this License.

2. VERBATIM COPYING

You may copy and distribute the Document in any medium, either commercially or noncommercially, provided that this License, the copyright notices, and the license notice saying this License applies to the Document are reproduced in all copies, and that you add no other conditions whatsoever to those of this License. You may not use technical measures to obstruct or control the reading or further copying of the copies you make or distribute. However, you may accept compensation in exchange for copies. If you distribute a large enough number of copies you must also follow the conditions in section 3.

You may also lend copies, under the same conditions stated above, and you may publicly display copies.

3. COPYING IN QUANTITY

If you publish printed copies (or copies in media that commonly have printed covers) of the Document, numbering more than 100, and the Document's license notice requires Cover Texts, you must enclose the copies in covers that carry, clearly and legibly, all these Cover Texts: Front-Cover Texts on the front cover, and Back-Cover Texts on the back cover. Both covers must also clearly and legibly identify you as the publisher of these copies. The front cover must present the full title with all words of the title equally prominent and visible. You may add other material on the covers in addition. Copying with changes limited to the covers, as long as they preserve the title of the Document and satisfy these conditions, can be treated as verbatim copying in other respects.

If the required texts for either cover are too voluminous to fit legibly, you should put the first ones listed (as many as fit reasonably) on the actual cover, and continue the rest onto adjacent pages.

If you publish or distribute Opaque copies of the Document numbering more than 100, you must either include a machine-readable Transparent copy along with each Opaque copy, or state in or with each Opaque copy a computer-network location from which the general network-using public has access to download using public-standard network protocols a complete Transparent copy of the Document, free of added material. If you use the latter option, you must take reasonably prudent steps, when you begin distribution of Opaque copies in quantity, to ensure that this Transparent copy will remain thus accessible at the stated location until at least one year after the last time you distribute an Opaque copy (directly or through your agents or retailers) of that edition to the public.

It is requested, but not required, that you contact the authors of the Document well before redistributing any large number of copies, to give them a chance to provide you with an updated version of the Document.

4. MODIFICATIONS

You may copy and distribute a Modified Version of the Document under the conditions of sections 2 and 3 above, provided that you release the Modified Version under precisely this License, with the Modified Version filling the role of the Document, thus licensing distribution and modification of the Modified Version to whoever possesses a copy of it. In addition, you must do these things in the Modified Version:

- A. Use in the Title Page (and on the covers, if any) a title distinct from that of the Document, and from those of previous versions (which should, if there were any, be listed in the History section of the Document). You may use the same title as a previous version if the original publisher of that version gives permission.

- B. List on the Title Page, as authors, one or more persons or entities responsible for authorship of the modifications in the Modified Version, together with at least five of the principal authors of the Document (all of its principal authors, if it has fewer than five), unless they release you from this requirement.

- C. State on the Title page the name of the publisher of the Modified Version, as the publisher.

- D. Preserve all the copyright notices of the Document.

- E. Add an appropriate copyright notice for your modifications adjacent to the other copyright notices.

- F. Include, immediately after the copyright notices, a license notice giving the public permission to use the Modified Version under the terms of this License, in the form shown in the Addendum below.

- G. Preserve in that license notice the full lists of Invariant Sections and required Cover Texts given in the Document's license notice.

- H. Include an unaltered copy of this License.

- I. Preserve the section Entitled "History", Preserve its Title, and add to it an item stating at least the title, year, new authors, and publisher of the Modified Version as given on the Title Page. If there is no section Entitled "History" in the Document, create one stating the title, year, authors, and publisher of the Document as given on its Title Page, then add an item describing the Modified Version as stated in the previous sentence.

- J. Preserve the network location, if any, given in the Document for public access to a Transparent copy of the Document, and likewise the network locations given in the Document for previous versions it was based on. These may be placed in the "History" section. You may omit a network location for a work that was published at least four years before the Document itself, or if the original publisher of the version it refers to gives permission.

- K. For any section Entitled "Acknowledgements" or "Dedications", Preserve the Title of the section, and preserve in the section all the substance and tone of each of the contributor acknowledgements and/or dedications given therein.

- L. Preserve all the Invariant Sections of the Document, unaltered in their text and in their titles. Section numbers or the equivalent are not considered part of the section titles.

- M. Delete any section Entitled "Endorsements". Such a section may not be included in the Modified Version.

- N. Do not retitle any existing section to be Entitled "Endorsements" or to conflict in title with any Invariant Section.

- O. Preserve any Warranty Disclaimers.

If the Modified Version includes new front-matter sections or appendices that qualify as Secondary Sections and contain no material copied from the Document, you may at your option designate some or all of these sections as invariant. To do this, add their titles to the list of Invariant Sections in the Modified Version's license notice. These titles must be distinct from any other section titles.

You may add a section Entitled "Endorsements", provided it contains nothing but endorsements of your Modified Version by various parties--for example, statements of peer review or that the text has been approved by an organization as the authoritative definition of a standard.

You may add a passage of up to five words as a Front-Cover Text, and a passage of up to 25 words as a Back-Cover Text, to the end of the list of Cover Texts in the Modified Version. Only one passage of Front-Cover Text and one of Back-Cover Text may be added by (or through arrangements made by) any one entity. If the Document already includes a cover text for the same cover, previously added by you or by arrangement made by the same entity you are acting on behalf of, you may not add another; but you may replace the old one, on explicit permission from the previous publisher that added the old one.

The author(s) and publisher(s) of the Document do not by this License give permission to use their names for publicity for or to assert or imply endorsement of any Modified Version.

5. COMBINING DOCUMENTS

You may combine the Document with other documents released under this License, under the terms defined in section 4 above for modified versions, provided that you include in the combination all of the Invariant Sections of all of the original documents, unmodified, and list them all as Invariant Sections of your combined work in its license notice, and that you preserve all their Warranty Disclaimers.

The combined work need only contain one copy of this License, and multiple identical Invariant Sections may be replaced with a single copy. If there are multiple Invariant Sections with the same name but different contents, make the title of each such section unique by adding at the end of it, in parentheses, the name of the original author or publisher of that section if known, or else a unique number. Make the same adjustment to the section titles in the list of Invariant Sections in the license notice of the combined work.

In the combination, you must combine any sections Entitled "History" in the various original documents, forming one section Entitled "History"; likewise combine any sections Entitled "Acknowledgements", and any sections Entitled "Dedications". You must delete all sections Entitled "Endorsements."

6. COLLECTIONS OF DOCUMENTS

You may make a collection consisting of the Document and other documents released under this License, and replace the individual copies of this License in the various documents with a single copy that is included in the collection, provided that you follow the rules of this License for verbatim copying of each of the documents in all other respects.

You may extract a single document from such a collection, and distribute it individually under this License, provided you insert a copy of this License into the extracted document, and follow this License in all other respects regarding verbatim copying of that document.

7. AGGREGATION WITH INDEPENDENT WORKS

A compilation of the Document or its derivatives with other separate and independent documents or works, in or on a volume of a storage or distribution medium, is called an "aggregate" if the copyright resulting from the compilation is not used to limit the legal rights of the compilation's users beyond what the individual works permit. When the Document is included in an aggregate, this License does not apply to the other works in the aggregate which are not themselves derivative works of the Document.

If the Cover Text requirement of section 3 is applicable to these copies of the Document, then if the Document is less than one half of the entire aggregate, the Document's Cover Texts may be placed on covers that bracket the Document within the aggregate, or the electronic equivalent of covers if the Document is in electronic form. Otherwise they must appear on printed covers that bracket the whole aggregate.

8. TRANSLATION

Translation is considered a kind of modification, so you may distribute translations of the Document under the terms of section 4. Replacing Invariant Sections with translations requires special permission from their copyright holders, but you may include translations of some or all Invariant Sections in addition to the original versions of these Invariant Sections. You may include a translation of this License, and all the license notices in the Document, and any Warranty Disclaimers, provided that you also include the original English version of this License and the original versions of those notices and disclaimers. In case of a disagreement between the translation and the original version of this License or a notice or disclaimer, the original version will prevail.

If a section in the Document is Entitled "Acknowledgements", "Dedications", or "History", the requirement (section 4) to Preserve its Title (section 1) will typically require changing the actual title.

9. TERMINATION

You may not copy, modify, sublicense, or distribute the Document except as expressly provided for under this License. Any other attempt to copy, modify, sublicense or distribute the Document is void, and will automatically terminate your rights under this License. However, parties who have received copies, or rights, from you under this License will not have their licenses terminated so long as such parties remain in full compliance.

10. FUTURE REVISIONS OF THIS LICENSE

The Free Software Foundation may publish new, revised versions of the GNU Free Documentation License from time to time. Such new versions will be similar in spirit to the present version, but may differ in detail to address new problems or concerns. See http://www.gnu.org/copyleft/.

Each version of the License is given a distinguishing version number. If the Document specifies that a particular numbered version of this License "or any later version" applies to it, you have the option of following the terms and conditions either of that specified version or of any later version that has been published (not as a draft) by the Free Software Foundation. If the Document does not specify a version number of this License, you may choose any version ever published (not as a draft) by the Free Software Foundation.

Addendum: How to use this License for your documents

To use this License in a document you have written, include a copy of the License in the document and put the following copyright and license notices just after the title page:

```
Copyright (c)  YEAR  YOUR NAME.
Permission is granted to copy, distribute and/or modify this document
under the terms of the GNU Free Documentation License, Version 1.2
or any later version published by the Free Software Foundation;
with no Invariant Sections, no Front-Cover Texts, and no Back-Cover Texts.
A copy of the license is included in the section entitled "GNU
Free Documentation License".
```

If you have Invariant Sections, Front-Cover Texts and Back-Cover Texts, replace the "with...Texts." line with this:

```
with the Invariant Sections being LIST THEIR TITLES, with the
Front-Cover Texts being LIST, and with the Back-Cover Texts being LIST.
```

If you have Invariant Sections without Cover Texts, or some other combination of the three, merge those two alternatives to suit the situation.

If your document contains nontrivial examples of program code, we recommend releasing these examples in parallel under your choice of free software license, such as the GNU General Public License, to permit their use in free software.

Index

We'd like to hear your suggestions for improving our indexes. Send email to *index@oreilly.com*.

functions
  built-in functions, XForms, 55–60
  built-in functions, XPath, 47–55
  extension functions, 60, 182
  (see also computed expressions)
functions attribute, <model>
      element, 82, 182

G

GET method, 11, 141, 142
getInstanceDocument() method, 180
"gHorribleKluge" datatypes, 76
GNU Free Documentation
      License, 194–202
graphical designer, role of, 166
greater than operator (>)
  in computed expression, 46
  in predicate, 37
greater than or equal to operator (>=), in
      computed expression, 46
<group> element, 27, 108

H

handler attribute, <listener>
      element, 117
handlers, 118
  (see also error handling events;
      XForms Actions)
<help> element, in form controls, 103,
      130
hidden controls, HTML forms, 8
  (see also disabled form controls;
      relevant property)
<hint> element, in form controls, 103,
      130
HLink, 34
host languages, for XForms, 32
href attribute, XHTML, 33
.htaccess file, 175
HTML+, 2
HTML forms, 1, 3
  buttons, 5
  checkboxes, 6, 11
  disabled controls, 10
  encoding formats, 11, 13
  error processing, 128
  file select control, 8
  hidden controls, 8
  history of, 2

initialization of controls, 10, 13
keyboard interface, 10
labels, 9
legends, 9
limitations of, 12
multi-line text input control, 3, 11
multiple-select menus, 7, 11
object controls, 9
password text input control, 4, 11
radio buttons, 5, 11
readonly controls, 10
reset control, 5
single-line text input control, 3, 11
single-select menus, 7, 11
submit control, 5
submitting data, 11
workflow patterns and, 13
http scheme, 141
https scheme, 141

I

IBM XML Forms Package, 93
id attribute, <bind> element, 88
ID attribute type, 23, 32
id() function, 48
IDREF binding, 88, 89
if() function, 55
image uploads, form control for, 94–96
IME (Input Method Editor), 105
includenamespaceprefixes attribute,
      <submission> element, 144,
      145, 149
incremental attribute, 108
indent attribute, <submission>
      element, 149
index attribute, setindex action, 124
index() function, 57, 112
index of repeat set, 57, 124
inequality operator (!=), in computed
      expression, 46
InfoPath (Microsoft), 185–193
infoset (see XML Information Set)
initialization of HTML forms
      controls, 10, 13
initialization stage of XForms
      processing, 127
<input> element, HTML forms, 3, 4, 5,
      6, 8
input form control, 31, 91

Input Method Editor (see IME)
inputmode attribute, in form
        controls, 105–106
in-range form controls, 153
:in-range property, 153
insert action, 31, 63, 122–123, 126
instance data, 20, 81
    adding nodes to, 134
    binding attributes referencing, 83
    binding to model item
        properties, 88–90
    creating new node in, 122–123
    <instance> element containing, 24,
        82
    interacting with form controls, 107
    "lazy author" processing
        providing, 81, 129
    as list selections, 101
    removing nodes from, 123, 134
    resetting, 121
    returning current state of, 180
    secondary, referencing, 27
    serializing, 144–147
    setting values in, 120
    submitting, 138–140, 148
    (see also nodes; node-set)
<instance> element, 24, 81, 82
    multiple, in one model, 26, 89, 138
instance() function, 27, 58, 90, 139
interaction events, 128, 130, 133, 134
interaction stage of XForms
        processing, 127
invalid form controls, 131, 153, 158
:invalid property, 153, 158
<itemset> element, select and select1
        form controls, 27, 101

J

Java applets, using in forms (see object
        controls)

K

keyboard events, 133
keyboard interface, HTML forms
        controls, 10
keyboard navigation, 169
keyboard shortcuts, 104

L

<label> element, 103
    HTML forms, 9
    output form control, 94
labels
    aligning, 156–158
    form controls, 94, 103
    HTML forms, 9
lang() function, 53
languages
    accepting input from non-native
        keyboards, 105–106
    determining for node, 53
    host, for XForms, 32
    localization and, 167–169
    right-to-left reading order, labels
        for, 157
    xs:language datatype for, 70
last() function, 47
"lazy author" processing, 17, 81, 129
<legend> element, HTML forms, 9
legends, HTML forms, 9
less than operator (<)
    in computed expression, 46
    in predicate, 37
less than or equal to operator (<=), in
        computed expression, 46
level attribute, message action, 119
lexical space for datatype, 64
lifecycle events, 128, 129, 134
linking
    attributes, 33
    errors/exceptions during, 136
    traversing a link, 121
listboxes (see single-select menus)
<listener> element, 117
listItems datatype, 66
lists
    datatypes for, 75
    initialization of, 11
    instance data providing selections
        for, 101
    multiple-select menus, 7
    open selection in, 17
    select and deselect events for, 131
    select form control, 100, 101
    select1 form control, 98, 101
    single-select menus, 7
load action, 121

About the Author

Micah Dubinko is a software engineer who lives in Phoenix, Arizona, with his wife and child, and works for Cardiff Software in San Diego. He serves as an editor and author of the W3C XForms specification, and has participated in the XForms effort since September 1999, nine months before the official Working Group was chartered. He was awarded CompTIA CDIA (Certified Document Imaging Architech) certification in January 2001.

Micah has been programming since the third grade, when he taught himself BASIC on a Timex/Sinclair computer with 2 KB of memory. Roughly in order, some of his on-the-job accomplishments have included designing and writing a 16-way multitasking communication server under DOS, porting biomed cardiac analysis software to Windows, redesigning the electronics in the frontend of a cardiac Holter monitor, debugging an embedded USB driver, writing a high-speed data entry system in MFC, spending time in product management, and, most recently, designing a cross-browser, plug-in-free transformation, and scripting framework for forms. In his spare time, Micah writes magazine articles and participates on *XMLhack.com* and *exslt.org*.

Colophon

Our look is the result of reader comments, our own experimentation, and feedback from distribution channels. Distinctive covers complement our distinctive approach to technical topics, breathing personality and life into potentially dry subjects.

The animal on the cover of *XForms Essentials* is a vulturine guinea fowl (*Acryillium vulturinum*). This African family of birds belongs to the same order as chachalacas, chickens, curassows, grouse, guans, hoatzins, mesites, partridges, pheasants, quail, and turkeys. Sometimes called the Royal guinea fowl—as the tallest and most colorful species of its genus—the vulturine guinea fowl earned its name because of its vulture-like head and neck, while its plumage sports black and white dots and stripes on a background of lilac and cobalt blue.

Vulturine guinea fowl breed well, producing a clutch of four to eight eggs, and laying several clutches if the eggs disappear. After the eggs hatch, the male feeds and protects the chicks for the first few days.

Vulturine guinea fowl thrive in the heat and bright sun of eastern Africa, spending their days foraging primarily in open dry scrublands for grasses, leaves, and other green vegetation. This diet provides them with nearly all of the moisture they require, allowing them to survive for long periods without water. These tall birds—24 inches (60 centimeters) in height—are easily spotted walking through the brush, usually in flocks of 20 to 25 birds, but regularly seen in flocks of 70. In the right conditions, they will consume enormous quantities of insects and also dine on berries and seeds. A flock of vulturine guinea fowl generally escapes from predators by running swiftly, flying only as a last resort. However, the flock also flies when it roosts in trees at nightfall, when the otherwise quiet birds make their characteristic cry, which resembles creaking wagon wheels.

The ancient Greeks and Romans domesticated these birds, and guinea fowl even figure in a Greek myth. When the hero Meleager (whose name means guinea fowl) was slain—after defending the honor of the huntress Atalanta—the goddess Artemis turned his sisters Gorge and Deianira (the wife of Heracles) into guinea fowl, which Artemis considered her sacred birds. However, the god Dionysus begged Artemis to return the two women (known as the Meleagrids) to their human form, and she did.

Reg Aubry was the production editor and copyeditor for *XForms Essentials*. Derek Di Matteo was the proofreader. Claire Cloutier provided quality control. James Quill, Jessamyn Read, and Julie Hawks provided production assistance. Angela Howard wrote the index.

Ellie Volckhausen designed the cover of this book, based on a series design by Edie Freedman. The cover image is a 19th-century engraving from the Dover Pictorial Archive. Emma Colby produced the cover layout with QuarkXPress 4.1 using Adobe's ITC Garamond font.

David Futato designed the interior layout. This book was converted by Joe Wizda to FrameMaker 5.5.6 with a format conversion tool created by Erik Ray, Jason McIntosh, Neil Walls, and Mike Sierra that uses Perl and XML technologies. The text font is Linotype Birka; the heading font is Adobe Myriad Condensed; and the code font is LucasFont's TheSans Mono Condensed. The illustrations that appear in the book were produced by Robert Romano and Jessamyn Read using Macromedia FreeHand 9 and Adobe Photoshop 6. The tip and warning icons were drawn by Christopher Bing. This colophon was written by Reg Aubry.

Other Titles Available from O'Reilly

XML

XML in a Nutshell, 2nd Edition

By Elliotte Rusty Harold &
W. Scott Means
1st Edition December 2000
400 pages, ISBN 0-596-00058-8

This powerful new edition provides developers with a comprehensive guide to the rapidly evolving XML space. Serious users of XML will find topics on just about everything they need, from fundamental syntax rules, to details of DTD and XML Schema creation, to XSLT transformations, to APIs used for processing XML documents. Simply put, this is the only reference of its kind among XML books.

XSLT Cookbook

By Sal Mangano
1st Edition December 2002
670 pages, ISBN 0-596-00372-2

This book offers the definitive collection of solutions and examples that developers at any level can use immediately to solve a wide variety of XML processing issues. As with our other Cookbook titles, *XSLT Cookbook* contains code recipes for specific programming problems. But more than just a book of cut and paste code, *XSLT Cookbook* enables developers to build their programming skills and their understanding of XSLT through the detailed explanations provided with each recipe.

Learning XML

By Erik T. Ray with
Christopher R. Maden
1st Edition January 2001
368 pages, ISBN 0-596-00046-4

XML (Extensible Markup Language) is a flexible way to create "self-describing data"—and to share both the format and the data on the World Wide Web, intranets, and elsewhere. In *Learning XML*, the authors explain XML and its capabilities succinctly and professionally, with references to real-life projects and other cogent examples. *Learning XML* shows the purpose of XML markup itself, the CSS and XSL styling languages, and the XLink and XPointer specifications for creating rich link structures.

XML Schema

By Eric van der Vlist
1st Edition June 2002
400 pages, 0-596-00252-1

The W3C's XML Schema offers a powerful set of tools for defining acceptable XML document structures and content. While schemas are powerful, that power comes with substantial complexity. This book explains XML Schema foundations, a variety of different styles for writing schemas, simple and complex types, datatypes and facets, keys, extensibility, documentation, design choices, best practices, and limitations. Complete with references, a glossary, and examples throughout.

XSLT

By Doug Tidwell
1st Edition August 2001
473 pages, ISBN 0-596-00053-7

XSLT (Extensible Stylesheet Language Transformations) is a critical bridge between XML processing and more familiar HTML, and dominates the market for conversions between XML vocabularies. Useful as XSLT is, its complexities can be daunting. Doug Tidwell, a developer with years of XSLT experience, eases the pain by building from the basics to the more complex and powerful possibilities of XSLT, so you can jump in at your own level of expertise.

Java & XML, 2nd Edition

By Brett McLaughlin
2nd Edition September 2001
528 pages, ISBN 0-596-00197-5

New chapters on Advanced SAX, Advanced DOM, SOAP, and data binding, as well as new examples throughout, bring the second edition of *Java & XML* thoroughly up to date. Except for a concise introduction to XML basics, the book focuses entirely on using XML from Java applications. It's a worthy companion for Java developers working with XML or involved in messaging, web services, or the new peer-to-peer movement.

O'REILLY®

To order: 800-998-9938 • order@oreilly.com • www.oreilly.com
Online editions of most O'Reilly titles are available by subscription at safari.oreilly.com
Also available at most retail and online bookstores.

XML

XSL-FO

By Dave Pawson
1st Edition August 2002
282 pages, ISBN 0-596-00355-2

This book offers in-depth coverage of XSL-FO's features. Unlike documentation from the World Wide Web Consortium (W3C)—the other primary source—all the material in *XSL-FO* is presented in a single coherent flow, without references to and changes of the Cascading Style Sheet (CSS) specification.

The XML CD Bookshelf

By O'Reilly & Associates, Inc.
Version 1.0 November 2002
640 pages, ISBN 0-596-00335-8

This unique CD collection is an XML developer's dream. Packed with seven popular O'Reilly books, The *XML CD Bookshelf* provides developers with a treasure trove of easily accessible and searchable XML information, all from the convenience of their computer's CD-ROM drive. Included are the latest unabridged versions *XML In a Nutshell*, 2nd Edition; *XSLT*; *XML Schema*; *SAX2*; *Java & XML*, 2nd Edition; *Java & XSLT*; and *Perl & XML*. As a bonus, we've included a print copy of *XML In a Nutshell*, 2nd Edition. Everything developers need to know about XML is literally at their fingertips.

Perl & XML

By Erik T. Ray & Jason McIntosh
1st Edition April 2002
216 pages, ISBN 0-596-00205-X

Perl & XML is aimed at Perl programmers who need to work with XML documents and data. This book gives a complete, comprehensive tour of the landscape of Perl and XML, making sense of the myriad of modules, terminology, and techniques. The last two chapters of Perl and XML give complete examples of XML applications, pulling together all the tools at your disposal.

XPath and XPointer

By John E. Simpson
1st Edition August 2002
208 pages, ISBN 0-596-00291-2

This hands-on book fills an essential need for XML developers by dealing with a topic that has been addressed inadequately up until now. *Xpath and Xpointer* offers practical knowledge on the two languages that underpin XML, XSLT, and Xlink. By referencing parts of documents, both Xpath and Xpointer play a key role in XML processing, allowing developers to manipulate embedded information. This book is packed with examples that demonstrate exactly how to use Xpath in different situations, showing developers a clear path for working with XML documents.

Java and XSLT

By Eric M. Burke
1st Edition September 2001
528 pages, ISBN 0-596-00143-6

Learn how to use XSL transformations in Java programs ranging from stand-alone applications to servlets. *Java and XSLT* introduces XSLT and then shows you how to apply transformations in real-world situations, such as developing a discussion forum, transforming documents from one form to another, and generating content for wireless devices.

Python & XML

By Christopher A. Jones
& Fred Drake
1st Edition December 2001
378 pages, ISBN 0-596-00128-2

This book has two objectives: to provide a comprehensive reference on using XML with Python and to illustrate the practical applications of these technologies (often coupled with cross-platform tools) in an enterprise environment. Loaded with practical examples, it also shows how to use Python to create scalable XML connections between popular distributed applications such as databases and web servers. Covers XML flow analysis and details ways to transport XML through a network.

O'REILLY®

To order: *800-998-9938* • *order@oreilly.com* • *www.oreilly.com*
Online editions of most O'Reilly titles are available by subscription at *safari.oreilly.com*
Also available at most retail and online bookstores.

How to stay in touch with O'Reilly

1. Visit our award-winning web site

http://www.oreilly.com/

★ "Top 100 Sites on the Web"—PC Magazine
★ CIO Magazine's Web Business 50 Awards

Our web site contains a library of comprehensive product information (including book excerpts and tables of contents), downloadable software, background articles, interviews with technology leaders, links to relevant sites, book cover art, and more. File us in your bookmarks or favorites!

2. Join our email mailing lists

Sign up to get email announcements of new books and conferences, special offers, and O'Reilly Network technology newsletters at:

http://elists.oreilly.com

It's easy to customize your free elists subscription so you'll get exactly the O'Reilly news you want.

3. Get examples from our books

To find example files for a book, go to:

http://www.oreilly.com/catalog

select the book, and follow the "Examples" link.

4. Work with us

Check out our web site for current employment opportunites:

http://jobs.oreilly.com/

5. Register your book

Register your book at:

http://register.oreilly.com

6. Contact us

O'Reilly & Associates, Inc.
1005 Gravenstein Hwy North
Sebastopol, CA 95472 USA
TEL: 707-827-7000 or 800-998-9938
          (6am to 5pm PST)
FAX: 707-829-0104

order@oreilly.com
For answers to problems regarding your order or our products. To place a book order online visit:

http://www.oreilly.com/order_new/

catalog@oreilly.com
To request a copy of our latest catalog.

booktech@oreilly.com
For book content technical questions or corrections.

corporate@oreilly.com
For educational, library, government, and corporate sales.

proposals@oreilly.com
To submit new book proposals to our editors and product managers.

international@oreilly.com
For information about our international distributors or translation queries. For a list of our distributors outside of North America check out:

http://international.oreilly.com/distributors.html

adoption@oreilly.com
For information about academic use of O'Reilly books, visit:

http://academic.oreilly.com

O'REILLY®